White Faculty at HBCUs

Moron . Martyr . Messiah . Marginal Man

Perceptions of Racial Climate

SaFiya D. Hoskins, Ph.D.

DEDICATION

To my father, David Earl Hoskins, who taught me to be aware of the varying levels (or perspectives) from which people articulate their comprehension of the Universe. He challenged me daily to communicate and act, always, from a place of love and compassion.

CONTENTS

Ubiquitous Press

ACKNOWLEDGEMENTS

To the casual observer, research and writing may appear to be a solitary endeavor. However, to complete a project of this magnitude, requires a network of support, and I am indebted to many people.

Dr. Neari F. Warner, the quintessential 'old school English teacher' and illustrious first female president of Grambling State University, I am grateful for your assiduous and meticulous attention to my manuscript. I am inspired by your professional poise and assertiveness. It is an honor and a privilege to have worked under your guidance.

Dr. Barbara J. Johnson, the impetus behind my explorations on the topic white faculty perceptions of racial climate at HBCUs, for me you opened up a new world. Thank you for trusting a neophyte with your work, your name and your research. I am grateful for your uncompromising candor and spirit.

Dr. Joseph Martin Stevenson, consummate 'catalyst for change,' I endeavor to honor your accomplishments and your efforts by following the example you have set for African American scholars to transform those deprived communities in our nation from bastions of hopelessness to citadels of promise.

Dr. Wynetta Y. Lee, a highly recognized and esteemed academician, thank you for your time, nurturing and fresh perspective on the use of quantitative methodology.

I would also like to acknowledge, Dr. Derek C. Henson, Dr. Leonard Williams and L. Kahlil Gross.

My eternal gratitude to Dr. George Tony French, Jr. for articulating his vision; today a prophecy fulfilled. I owe my doctorate to your unyielding zeal, fastidious direction and unrelenting support.

To my godchildren, Shayne Hale-Malone, Darell Foote, Ostin Taylor and Rohan Walton thank you for your unconditional love and maturity when the rigors of research did not allow for our usual exchanges and outings. Presenting for you the highest standard from which our legacy must continue, an example for you to live by, is always foremost. You are all my future, my heart.

Your hearts know in silence the secrets of the days and nights.
But your ears thirst for the sound of your heart's knowledge.
You would know in words that which you have always known in thought.
You would touch with your fingers the naked body of your dreams.

KAHLIL GIBRAN
on 'Self-Knowledge' from *The Prophet* (1923)

1 WHY DO WHITE FACULTY PERSPECTIVES AT HBCUS MATTER?

INTRODUCTION

Stakeholders' perceptions can influence and be influenced by racial climate in an organization, particularly when the minority population comprises members of a historically hegemonic class. As such, interpretation becomes a matter of power or authority to determine morality and meaning. Moreover, the intersubjectivity of interracial work relationships could influence satisfaction and productivity within an environment. Consequently, studies at historically White institutions (HWIs) have revealed an environment that is perceived as hostile and alienating by students and faculty of color. As the number of White faculty at Historically Black Colleges and Universities (HBCUs) is significant, it might therefore be reasonably assumed that studies on this phenomenon are readily available. Quite to the contrary, there is limited empirical research on White faculty at HBCUs, particularly regarding their perceptions of racial climate. As a result, this study seeks to explore questions of how White faculty perceive the racial climate at HBCUs.

Current studies on White faculty at HBCUs have found that they were paid lower wages, assigned subordinate roles, and were viewed as inferior. A number of these faculty were observed as having feelings of insecurity associated with rejection and characteristics of vulnerability. In a study conducted by Warnat (1976), it was suggested that White faculty at HBCUs could be classified as incompetent, unconscious of issues regarding Black people, and working at these institutions to relieve the guilt associated with racism. In a 1999 study on White faculty Foster, Guyden and Miller

5

reported their positive experiences at HBCUs. More specifically, perceived support from colleagues and students was indicated by White faculty at HBCUs as an important part of assimilation. Researchers concur that the variance among experiences of White faculty at HBCUs is vast. In an effort to provide additional insight into the phenomenon of White faculty at HBCUs, this study will explore the perceptions White faculty have of the racial climate at HBCUs.

Historically Blacks Colleges and Universities (HBCUs) have always welcomed diversity among their faculty ranks. According to a 2006 National Center for Educational Statistics report, there is a 6% Black faculty presence at HWIs compared to a 31% White and other faculty presence at HBCUs. There is a wealth of information about HWIs, in general, and White faculty, in particular; yet, few studies, by comparison, have been conducted about HBCUs or White faculty at HBCUs. Even fewer are those studies on the perceptions of White faculty at HBCUs, and almost three decades have passed since those few were introduced. There exists a void in the literature on White faculty at HBCUs, in general, and White faculty perceptions of racial climate at HBCUs, in particular.

Although Warnat conducted research on White faculty at HBCUs in 1976, nine years before the emergence of the Smith and Borgstedt study in 1985, both studies evidenced perceptions of supremacy, dominance, and questions of competence by White faculty at HBCUs. Racial climate is a sociological construct that can affect relationships, satisfaction, productivity, and morale in an environment. Examining White faculty perceptions of racial climate at HBCUs is critical to addressing interpretive factors relative to personal, relational and organizational effectiveness on HBCU campuses.

This study will address a void in the literature on HBCUs relative to faculty perceptions of racial climate. Specifically, research will be devoted to White faculty perceptions of racial climate at HBCUs: how and why they are formed, reinforced or changed. Perceptions are the result of one's past experiences, respective culture and subjective interpretation of the perceived. Dr. Cornel West illustrates in *Race Matters* (1993) what history has shown repeatedly: White and Black experiences in America often differ; their cultures vary, and their subsequent analysis of observations and experiences frequently diverge. Examining White faculty perceptions of racial climate at HBCUs is critical to inspiring dialogue on interracial dynamics relative to social and professional relationships on HBCU campuses.

The primary research question of this study is: How do White faculty at HBCUs perceive racial climate? The secondary research questions are as follows:

    1.   How do they perceive the professional atmosphere at HBCUs?

2. How do they perceive the culture of HBCUs?
3. How do their perceptions of HBCUs change after starting employment at an HBCU?

Research on HBCUs, in general, is limited, necessitating additional knowledge. Exploring the perceptions of White faculty at HBCUs gives insight into an often overlooked population at HBCUs. Many White faculty are motivated to work at HBCUs because of the current competitive market for employment in higher education, a phenomenon that needs to be documented.

Information on White faculty perceptions at HBCUs is limited and outdated. It should not be assumed that White faculty perceptions of HBCUs' relevance almost 30 years ago hold true today. This study is significant because it grants a voice to White faculty who are often unheard in research on HBCUs. Moreover, it will provide the reader with current knowledge on perceptions of White faculty at HBCUs.

Researchers may be prompted, by this study, to explore the perceptions of other minority populations at HBCUs, namely African, Asian, Hispanic and international faculty. Enhanced perceptions by faculty at varying institutions regardless of ethnicity and gender can be garnered by utilizing a framework that describes the perception process, thereby optimizing both sense-making and the sense we make.

This study may be of value to a number of groups. White students considering careers as HBCU faculty might confront their perceptions for the sake of optimizing the employment process and experience. White HBCU faculty might re-examine their perceptions for insight into their past, present and future experiences. HBCU administrators might utilize this study as a guide for understanding White faculty perceptions of HBCUs as part of enhancing the experiences for the aforementioned and those with whom they come in contact. Finally, HWIs might generalize these findings on perceptions of racial climate to begin cultivating a diverse institutional culture that acknowledges, invites and welcomes faculty on campus both in policy and practice.

Two private HBCUs will be selected as sites for this study. In particular, one institution is large, urban, secular and situated in the North, while the other institution is small, rural, religiously affiliated and situated in the South. Characteristics of faculty participants will include the following: White, full-time, tenured faculty. Utilizing a qualitative data collection approach, information pertaining to the perceptions of White faculty at HBCUs will be gathered. Participants will be selected using a criterion sample method. Interviews will be audio recorded and transcribed verbatim based on the guidelines established by Miles and Huberman. By keeping field notes, the researcher will be able to recollect dialog, body language, events, and tones.

The delimitations of this study include the singular implementation of qualitative methods and a focus on White, full-time, tenured faculty. The sample sites present another delimitation in the study, particularly as only two HBCUs were selected from which to collect samples. Furthermore, these sites are located in just two regions. While this study will examine White faculty perceptions of racial climate, culture and professional atmosphere, it necessarily excludes close scrutiny of other interpretive, yet, pertinent factors influencing and influenced by perception.

The limitations of this study are presented by examining only a small sample of White faculty from two HBCUs, making it difficult to generalize the findings. However, by selecting two institutions with diversified characteristics located in discrete regions, the opportunity for wide-ranging participant responses is enhanced. Another limitation is the possibility that fear for their professional livelihood may impede the willingness of White faculty to participate in the study. Yet, by using only tenured faculty participants, they may feel assured of the unlikelihood for professional repercussions. Finally, the race of the researcher may serve as a limitation in conducting interviews with White faculty who may feel uncomfortable answering questions concerning race in said presence. Nonetheless, informal and structured assurances in the form of greetings and a review of confidentiality documents proceeded by professional decorum during interviews may help to impede any feelings of discomfort on the part of respondents.

The key terms listed below have been operationalized to provide the reader with knowledge of the researcher's intended definition of the terms throughout the study:

> *Culture* refers to the conventional belief system, attitudes, and norms that any given group (of faculty members) might embrace.

> *Historically Black Colleges and Universities* (HBCUs) are accredited institutions of higher education in the United States established after the American Civil War and before 1964 for the purpose of educating African American students.

> *Historically White Institutions* (HWIs) are accredited institutions of higher education in the United States that were, at their inception, legally authorized to prohibit the enrollment of Blacks and other minorities prior to the Brown vs. The Board of Education (1954) ruling that separate is not equal.

Perception is the process by which individuals come to understand or grasp mentally or become aware by way of the senses.
Racial climate refers to the atmosphere or environment existing between races.

Tenure is a contractual agreement between an institution and faculty member identifying and guaranteeing the aforementioned of lifelong employment.

White refers to people with exclusively European ancestry.

The hidden well-spring of your soul must
needs rise and run murmuring to the sea;
And the treasure of your infinite depths
would be revealed to your eyes.

KAHLIL GIBRAN
on 'Self-Knowledge' from *The Prophet* (1923)

2 HWI VS. HBCU

Given the historical corollary between race and privilege in the United States, it is reasonably expected that White faculty would prefer to work at a Historically White Institution (HWIs) rather than a Historically Black College or University (HBCUs). Contrary to this socio-psychological phenomenon, disenfranchised White women and persecuted European scholars in the 1930s found an intellectual domicile at many HBCUs, all of which have been historically convivial to all races. Interestingly, current HBCU statistics report that nearly half of HBCU faculty is White and other. However, relatively few studies have been conducted to determine perceptions of racial climate by White faculty at HBCUs. Thus, this study seeks to discover how White faculty perceive racial climate at HBCUs, professional atmosphere and culture, and how their perceptions of HBCUs change after commencing employment at an HBCU.

At present, White and other faculty collectively comprise the percentage of faculty on HBCU campuses once represented by White faculty alone. Specifically, in 1977, White faculty at HBCUs numbered 40% but only 28% by 1981. On the contrary, international faculty at HBCUs have grown in number from only 5% in 1977 to 13% in 1995 and 15% in 2001. According to the most recent statistics available from the National Center for Education Statistics, in Fall 2001, the racial composition of faculty at HBCUs was 59% Black, 26% White and 15% other. Furthermore, NCES reports that 27% of the tenure- track positions at HBCUs are held by White faculty compared to only 16% by all minorities at HWIs.

Literature examining the evolution of faculty as a profession and their active presence on university campuses has traditionally referred specifically to White faculty at-large and HWIs. However, little research exists on the experiences of White faculty at Historically Black Colleges and Universities. Even fewer are the number of studies that explore the topic of racial climate. This study will provide indicators for understanding White faculty's reasons for choosing to work at an HBCU, their experiences, and the social and psychological dimensions of their interactions. Furthermore, there have evolved a number of frameworks from which to explore the social and psychological factors surrounding the presence and experiences of White faculty at HBCUs.

THE HISTORY OF FACULTY

In the middle of the eighteenth century, teaching as a profession in the United States evolved. It was not until the end of the century that faculty became a permanent fixture as professors within a university. Faculty wages were low through the latter part of the twentieth century with university affiliation considered an honor and thereby compensation enough.

At the beginning of the nineteenth century, the professionalization of faculty was developing. Also, professorial ranks emerged as merit was given to specialization and education within the profession. During this period, faculty generally came from nonacademic occupations. Many were encouraged to study in Germany and returned to the United States "with Germanic notions of the professor as an independent researcher" who provided guidance to students in specific instead of general subjects. A number of published works likened more to lectures surfaced during this era as a precursor to widely available research.

Large philanthropic gifts during what Cohen termed the "University Transformation Era" (1870-1944) made it possible for the wealthier universities to travel the country and seek out the best and brightest professors. Teaching and research hours varied between institutions with those possessing graduate departments also owning the specialists. Less classroom time was required of specialist at affluent institutions compared to faculty at less well-off institutions with only undergraduate programs. Existence of the previous at an institution brought prestige and sabbatical leaves so that professors could take paid leave for research purposes. In 1915, the American Association of University Professors (AAUP) was created to protect and advance the rights of faculty. It was popular at prestigious institutions for faculty to be chosen from among the doctoral graduates at their respective university. It also became prevalent for faculty to select incoming students.

The evolution of faculty as a profession in colleges and universities across the United States was a slow, yet steady, progression in the decades preceding 1945. The end of World War II would mark the beginning of what Cohen calls "education's golden age" with all the system's characteristics growing swiftly and being redefined in the process. However, it was the enactment of the GI Bill in 1944, formally referred to as the Serviceman's Readjustment Act, that catapulted higher education into an era of bountiful treasures. The GI Bill provided for a substantial portion of the previously uneducated populace to attend institutions of higher education, namely veterans of World War II. As a result of this opportunity, student enrollment increased nationwide, thus demanding the presence and attention of qualified faculty.

Exhibiting a striking and distinct start toward new trends in education coupled with the unveiling of new campuses nationwide, the years from 1945 through 1975 would witness the changing face of students and curricula. Evenmore, the professionalization of faculty could be quantified by the tides of development in favor of their vocation.

Although this 'golden age' of education beheld a wealth of progress, there would be a multiplicity of factors that would serve to rain on the parade of advancement. Heightening in the 1970s, perceptions of faculty would be thwarted by their move toward unionization, the system of tenure, the increase in qualified faculty, and faculty participation in rampant student protests. Prior to this cramp in the public's opinion of faculty, the profession had been revered for its prestige and exclusivity.

The number of faculty between 1940 and 1975 increased by 415,000, thereby boosting the average number of faculty per institution by 114 in the same time. The number of women faculty grew by 13% while the previously unmentionable number of minority faculty had risen to a still small, yet recognizable, 8%. The 'golden age' of education also saw a decrease in the median age of faculty.

Across the nation, faculty differ in orientation by discipline and institutional affiliation. "Cosmopolitans are faculty whose peers are colleagues across the country-or the world- who share specialized scholarly interests." For cosmopolitan faculty, home institutions merely serve as a foundation from which to work on their external publications and activities. On the other hand, locals are greatly committed to their campuses with an emphasis on community integration, teaching and institutional activities.

The 'golden age' in education witnessed integration of faculty that had been previously resisted on both the grounds of societal norms and legislation depriving academia of a substantial amount of knowledge owned by the marginalized.

According to Cohen, institutional diversity was due largely in part to the expansion of Title VII of the Civil Rights Act of 1964 in the year 1972: … to forbid discrimination in employment on the basis of race, color, religion, sex, or national origin in public and private educational institutions.

While progress was made to integrate the professoriate, efforts to provide security and legitimacy to the profession proliferated giving rise to faculty unions. These unions would emerge as full-time faculty at private institutions of higher education had been recognized as employees with the 1971 addendum by the National Labor Relations Board to the 1935 National Labor Relations Act, thereby giving them license to organize and unionize. Collective bargaining became a task of organizations such as the American Federation of Teachers and The American Association of University Professors with their memberships growing exponentially in the period after the addendum.

Faculty made grand strides during this era to secure control over decision-making in higher education on the doorsteps of their home institutions, even lobbying all the way to state capitals to participate in educational policy formulation and verdicts. Faculty emerged from 'the golden age' well-paid with a leverage before unknown.

The latter part of the 1970s brought more female faculty, part-time faculty and increased salaries. Female faculty were underrepresented at research institutions and overrepresented at community colleges. The strides for women at prestigious institutions were still, however, larger and faster than those for minorities. Between 1976 and 1998, several court cases would surface, some ruled on by the Supreme Court, addressing concerns of faculty nationwide including- but not limited to: unionization (National Labor Relations Board vs. Yeshiva University, 1980); academic freedom (Bishop vs. Aronov, 1991 and Levin vs. Harleston 1992); a researcher's right not to reveal his results (Dow Chemical vs. Allen, 1982); and age discrimination (Leftwich vs. Harris-Stowe College, 1983).

Let there be no scales to weigh your unknown treasure;
And seek not the depths of your knowledge with staff or sounding line.
For self is a sea boundless and measureless.

KAHLIL GIBRAN
on 'Self-Knowledge' from *The Prophet* (1923)

3 WHITES AND THE INCEPTION OF HBCUS

WHITE EFFORTS IN THE HISTORICAL EVOLUTION OF HBCUS

Contributions to HBCUs for the education and advancement of Black students were primarily generated from missionary groups, such as the American Missionary Association (AMA), the Freedmen's Aid Society of the Methodist Episcopal Church, the American Baptist Home Missionary Society (ABHMS), the Presbyterian Board of Missions for Freedmen, as well as independent northern missionaries.

There are numerous institutions owing their existence to the AMA like Fisk University, Straight University (Dillard) and Tougaloo College, and Talladega College. The Freedmen's Aid Society of the Methodist Episcopal Church also founded multiple institutions, including, Clark University, Bennett College, Claflin College, Meharry Medical College, Morgan State University, Philander Smith College, Rust College, and Wiley College. The Presbyterian Board of Missions for Freedman established Biddle University (now Johnson C. Smith), Knoxville College, Stillman Seminary, and Mary Allen Seminary. Atlanta University, Howard University, and Leland University were among those institutions established by independent northern missionary boards.

Thelin is among those researchers who chronicle that denominational missionary interest in Black education was based on the philosophy that they were responsible to "Christianize and educate the former slave," (Anderson, 1988, p. 457), believing that "without education...blacks would rapidly degenerate and become a national menace to American civilization," (Heintze, 1999, p. 1).

In the late nineteenth and early twentieth century, the prevailing opinion among Whites was that if Blacks were going to be educated, they should be trained in service and industry. The divergent opinion was of those who advocated the need for Black leadership in their communities and argued that industrial education would not facilitate the intellectual development critical for this role. Corresponding to the latter opinion, the AMA set about establishing institutions for exceptional Black youth with a classical liberal arts education equivalent to that offered at White institutions.

Well into the twentieth century, many Whites were violently against Black students acquiring a liberal arts education. According to Urban and Wagoner, a large percentage of the White population believed that Blacks were not equipped intellectually for such learning while others feared that too many more Blacks would want the intellectual emancipation that came from pursuing a liberal arts education.

The White industrial philanthropists, as proponents supportive of a subservient curriculum for blacks, included Peabody, Slater, Rosenwald, Andrew Carnegie, and the John D. Rockefellers, Sr. and Jr. Industrial philanthropists were rich and successfully advanced their institutions while organizations for classical liberal arts education sometimes struggled to maintain their institutions without subsidy from the aforementioned.

Despite evident difficulties, many Black institutions began to adopt the liberal arts curriculum for the obvious social and intellectual benefit for students. Whites debated both the curriculum and the leadership at Black liberal arts institutions. Many Whites did not approve of Blacks being placed in administrative positions and, consequently, withheld endorsements until the Great Depression forced financial constraints which limited selectivity.

As stated in the article, The Tradition of White Presidents at Black Colleges (1997), "[t]he White founders and supporters of the black colleges were reluctant to entrust control of the institutions to black people" (p. 93). It was not until 1926 that Mordecai Johnson became the first Black president of Howard University, an HBCU that was established by The Freedman's Bureau in 1867.

THE BACKGROUND OF WHITE FACULTY AT HBCUS

Historically black colleges and universities (HBCUs) have a historical legacy of inclusion. At the very root of their foundation is the notion of equal opportunity for everyone regardless of race, creed, color or national origin. HBCUs are attracting White faculty today for a variety of reasons, among them, increased employment opportunities and aggressive diversity recruitment strategies; however, little is known about the reasons that White faculty choose to work at HBCUs. According to the 2006 Cooper, Massey & Graham study "Being Dixie," forty-five percent of HBCU faculty is made up of Whites and other minorities including individuals from other countries.

> Dixie Massey confessed in her 2006 work with Cooper and Graham:
>
> I knew that I needed assistance not only in teaching a population of students that I had never taught before, but also in understanding the social mores of a historically Black college campus (p. 117).

It is evidenced by Cooper et. al. (2006) that socialization and perception dramatically influence respective experiences of White faculty, and subsequently their students.

The number of White faculty at HBCUs decreased from 40% in 1977 to 28% in 1981. Their percentage has since remained stable in the range of 26% to 29%. In contrast, faculty of other racial groups (Asian, Hispanic, American Indian, International) have increased from 5% in 1977 to 13% in 1995 to 15% in 2001. According the most recent available NCES data, in 2001 White faculty had a 26% presence at HBCUs and held 27% of the tenure-track positions. In total, the racial composition of faculty at HBCUs is 59% Black, 26% White and 15% other.

Considering the significant role of Whites in the inception of HBCUs, one might assume that there would be a plethora of literature on White faculty at Black colleges. A review of publications reveals quite the opposite. There is a lack of research on faculty at HBCUs in general and even fewer studies conducted on White faculty at HBCUs in particular. The few existent studies on White Faculty at HBCUs are outdated.

Say not, "I have found the truth," but
rather, "I have found a truth."
Say not, "I have found the path of the soul."
Say rather, "I have met the soul walking upon my path."

KAHLIL GIBRAN
on 'Self-Knowledge' from *The Prophet* (1923)

4 CLASSIFYING WHITE FACULTY AT HBCUS

WARNAT: A PIONEER

Winifred I. Warnat pioneered research on White Faculty experiences at HBCUs in his 1976 study, 'The Role of White Faculty on the Black Campus.' Warnat's research sought to classify White faculty upon entry into HBCUs according to a concept espoused by Ralph Linton that "each individual has a series of roles which come from numerous patterns in which the individual participates," (p. 335). The study found that White faculty were at odds with the culture at HBCUs as they struggled to assimilate into the HBCU community at the same time maintaining their hegemony, yet attempting to minimize their status as outsiders. White faculty who worked at HBCUs were categorized as assuming roles identified by Warnat as, the Moron (incompetence), Martyr (racial guilt), Messiah (savior) and Marginal Man (conflict over status as a White person working at an HBCU).

MORON.

The moron is essentially rejected by the White hegemony for assuming the supposed inferior status of working at an HBCU. Warnat explains, White faculty at HBCUs are perceived as incompetent and unable to perform according to the standards of their White counterparts employed at HWIs. It is reasoned that the moron chooses to remain working in the "negative environment" at an HBCU rather than confront his/her "fear of rejection" and acknowledge "the reality of limited ability," (Warnat, 1976). White faculty in this classification are inclined to blame their inadequacy on the alleged shortcomings of the Black institution where they are employed.

MARTYR.

The martyr is identified as the White faculty member who seeks to atone for the ills of his slaveholding ancestors and racist contemporaries by acting as something of a goodwill missionary. Engaging in laborious acts of servitude on the HBCU campus, the martyrs believe their suffering to be justified. Consistent with this self-denigrating attitude the martyrs disregard their potential aptitude and suppress any aspirations for achieving higher status on campus. Black faculty prefer to work with the martyr for whom they commiserate with for their perceived altruistic behavior.

MESSIAH.

The Messiah, as identified by Warnat, is the White faculty member who perceives his/her role on the HBCU campus as a social and intellectual emancipator on a mission to "save the damned" (p. 336). The presence of the White messiah on HBCU campuses is abhorred by Black faculty. According to Warnat (1976), "[m]ore than any other element of the White faculty, this one tends to foster mistrust and feelings of alienation and hostility among his colleagues towards him," (p. 336).

MARGINAL MAN.

The marginal man represents the White faculty member who finds it difficult to negotiate the historically privileged hegemonic status being reduced to a minority status on a majority Black HBCU campus. Reminiscent of Dubois' (1903) "duo consciousness" of the Black person in America navigating daily across cultures, Warnat describes the marginal White faculty member as traversing between the White community yet as an "alien" in the Black community due to a sense of White privilege and association with the hegemony. Although the White faculty member can "pass" on the historically inviting Black campus they are never fully assimilated due to their own cultural history, perpetually subject to their position as an outsider. Subsequently, the marginal man assigns him/herself to "the role he assumes in society" and "…the attitudes and opinions which members of the society form of him" (p. 337).

SMITH AND BORGSTEDT

Nearly a decade later, Smith and Borgstedt (1985) examined White faculty adjustment at six HBCUs. Their study found that sixty-six percent of White faculty at HBCUs felt powerless in decision making, occasional distrust by Black faculty, subject to an authoritarian administration and limited opportunities for advancement due to their race. Jacques' research on White faculty at HBCUs cites white faculty perceptions of "lower pay, inferior status and subordinate authority." A Roebuck and Murty study showed that White faculty at HBCUs perceived an "opportunity structure" that was strategically advantageous for Black faculty. Likewise, Roebuck and Murty found Black faculty's at HWIs perceptions of the "opportunity structure" exclusively beneficial to their White counterparts. Smith and Borgstedt discovered that White faculty were keenly aware of the social and formal climate at HBCUs and left their respective institutions when they were unwilling to adapt. The 1985 study also reported White faculty perceptions of "cooperative professional relationships" with Black faculty citing less professional competition at HBCUs compared to that among White faculty at HWIs. Furthermore, White faculty members seeking employment at HWIs after leaving their respective HBCUs instead found dissatisfaction there due to the lack of a diverse faculty and questionable race relations. In addition, White faculty revealed that their primary satisfaction at HBCUs was derived from interaction with students. Comparatively, Smith and Borgstedt identified perceptions of positive experiences by White faculty at HBCUs that outweighed those of their Black counterparts employed at HWIs.

Consistent with Smith and Borgstedt's (1985) findings on White faculty perceptions of positive experiences at HBCUs, Foster, Guyden, and Miller (1999) identified White faculty perceptions of successful integration on their respective HBCU campuses as a result of the support received from their colleagues and students. Johnson and Harvey's (2002) study confirmed that "formal and informal colleague support is necessary for the effective socialization of new faculty" (p. 302). Furthermore, the study reported positive in-classroom experiences for White faculty at HBCUs, likely attributed to their position of dominion over their students versus their professional equivalency with Black faculty. While White faculty at HBCUs might perceive a level of belonging they can never fully become an insider within a Black majority. Taking into account the collective findings of the aforementioned studies, it can be assumed that the process and perceptions of assimilation by White faculty at HBCUs is owed more to their White cultural background and the historical corollary between race and privilege in the United States than the atmosphere and legacy at HBCUs.

For the soul walks upon all paths.
The soul walks not upon a line, neither
does it grow like a reed.
The soul unfolds itself, like a lotus of countless petals.

KAHLIL GIBRAN
on 'Self-Knowledge' from *The Prophet* (1923)

5 DIMENSIONS OF RACIAL CLIMTE

CONCEPTUAL FRAMEWORK

The conceptual framework that will be utilized for this study was adapted from the framework developed by Hurtado, Milem, Clayton-Pederson and Allen (1998). Although this framework was originally developed to assess the campus racial climate as it relates to the perceptions of students at HWIs, the components of the model provide the foundation for exploring the campus climate of White faculty in a predominantly black environment. Consequently, the Hurtado et. al. (1998) framework will be referred to as the Four Dimensions of Campus Climate framework for the intentions of this study (Johnson, Hoskins, Johnson, 2008). Dimension one of the Campus Climate framework (Johnson, Hoskins, Johnson, 2008) represents the institutional legacy of inclusion or exclusion while the second dimension is structural diversity in terms of the numerical representation of various racial/ethnic groups. The psychological climate, dimension three, depicts the perceptions and attitudes between and among groups. Intergroup relations on campus comprise the final behavioral dimension.

The institutional climate is influenced by the four dimensions of campus climate: (a) historical legacy, (b) structural diversity, (c) psychological, and (d) behavioral. Likewise, the four dimensions of campus climate are affected by the institutional climate. Collectively, the four dimensions of campus climate unite to shape the culture and atmosphere of the institution. The culture of an institution influences how faculty arrive at the norms and values needed to persist in their institution. Subsequently, faculty perceptions affect and are affected by the four dimensions of campus climate and thus, influence the institutional climate. In correlation, faculty perceptions of the four dimensions of campus climate are influenced by external factors such as cultural background or socio-political partiality and preconceptions. Additionally, institutional size, large, medium or small, as well as the location of the institution in a rural or urban setting or Northern or Southern city may impact organizational culture, thus influencing faculty perceptions. In summation, faculty perceptions both influence and are influenced by those factors that comprise the institutional climate but not without external predisposition(s).

DIMENSION ONE: HISTORICAL LEGACY OF INCLUSION OR EXCLUSION

HBCUs were formed to offer educational opportunities for Blacks who were previously prohibited from receiving a formal education resulting in a lack of Black teachers trained to teach, thus the overwhelming majority of faculty initially at these institutions were primarily White. Accordingly, the purpose of establishing HBCUs coupled with the financial and human resources of White missionaries documented a legacy of inclusion at HBCUs from their inception. Throughout their history, these institutions have welcomed students and faculty of all genders, races, nationalities, and religions.

DIMENSION TWO: STRUCTURAL DIVERSITY

Structural diversity is an important part of defining racial climate on a college campus. A broad distribution of faculty across racial and ethnic boundaries contributes to the social and cultural diversity of an institution. Underrepresentation of a group on campus can present distorted images or stereotypes, social stigma and subsequently cause "minority status stress." Equally vital to the perceptions of racial climate on a college campus is an institution's position on the importance of creating a "multicultural environment." Case and point, Hurtado et. al. found that institutions with a high level of commitment to diversity were able to quantify their dedication by numerical representations. An increase in structural diversity also means academic and social revolution on college campuses with the installation of programs and curriculum that address the newly diversified environment.

DIMENSION THREE: PSYCHOLOGICAL DIMENSION

The psychological dimension of the campus climate comprises perceptions of group interactions, institutional reactions to diversity, attitudes towards individuals from varying racial and ethnic backgrounds, feelings of alienation, and perceptions of racial conflict or discrimination.

26

Hurtado et. al. (1998) found that campus climate is viewed differently by racially and ethnically diverse stakeholders on campus. Likewise, an individual's position and power at an institution and their status as an "insider" or "outsider" can strongly influence their perceptions about racial climate on campus.

DIMENSION FOUR: BEHAVIORAL DIMENSION

The behavioral dimension of institutional climate encompasses interactions and relations on campus. More specifically, the fourth dimension relates to social interaction, interaction both between and among individuals from varying racial and ethnic backgrounds, and the quality of intergroup relations on campus. While Hurtado et. al. (1998) identify student involvement as central to their educational experience and retention, presumably White faculty involvement on campus is essential to their professional experience at an HBCU and continuance therein. Interracial contact has a significant influence on the perception of others, support for campus initiatives and professional outcomes. Those who have frequent social interaction with individuals from various racial and ethnic backgrounds are more likely to hold positive attitudes toward multiculturalism on campus than those who have infrequent social interactions with divergent populations. Likewise, racial awareness and sensitivity are directly related to conversant exchanges between White faculty at HBCUs and the majority population on campus. Furthermore, participation in racial and ethnically diverse activities promotes higher social involvement. Figure 1 displays the model adapted for White faculty perceptions of racial climate from the Four Dimensions of Racial Climate framework.

Figure 1 – Four Dimension of Campus Climate Model adapted from the framework, Four Dimensions of Racial Climate, developed by Johnson, Hoskins, Johnson (2008).

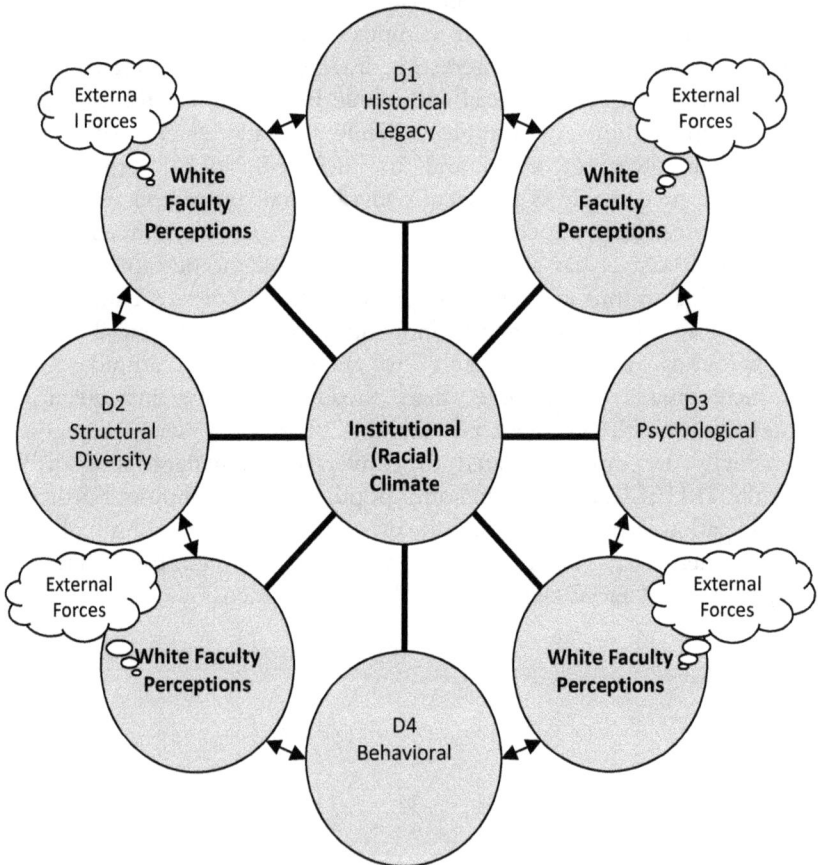

Your reason and your passion are the
rudder and the sails of your seafaring soul.
If either your sails or your rudder be
broken, you can but toss and drift, or else
be held at a standstill mid-seas.

KAHLIL GIBRAN
on 'Reason and Passion' from *The Prophet* (1923)

6 EXPLORING THE PHENOMENON

METHODOLOGY

Upon their entry into HBCUs, White faculty are immersed into an organizational culture divergent to the socio-political construction of the United States and reduced to existing at the institution as a minority in a majority Black populace. According to past research, the experiences and atmospheric observations of White faculty at HBCUs will vary according to their respective personal history and predispositions. Consequently, this study examined perceptions of White Faculty relative to racial climate at HBCUs.

Hence, this chapter provides the reader with an understanding of the methods implemented in this study to address the research questions. This chapter also reviews the rationale for qualitative methodology to explore the phenomenon. In addition, the process involved in the collection and analysis of the data is discussed. Finally, this chapter concludes with a discussion on the trustworthiness, delimitations, and limitations of the study.

The primary research question of this study is: How do White faculty at HBCUs perceive racial climate? The secondary research questions are as follows:

1. How do White faculty perceive the professional atmosphere at HBCUs?

2. How do White faculty perceive the diversity of HBCUs?

3. How do their perceptions of HBCUs change after starting employment at an HBCU?

RATIONALE FOR UTILIZING A QUALITATIVE RESEARCH APPROACH

The purpose of qualitative inquiry is "to produce depth of understanding from a particular topic or experience" (Manning, 1999, p. 12). A qualitative research design was utilized to gain an in-depth understanding of the perceptions of the racial climate as perceived by White faculty at historically black colleges and universities (HBCUs). Since little was known about faculty perceptions of the racial climate at HBCUs, their voices can best be presented through detailed examples or narratives. The qualitative approach permitted the researcher to determine meaning in the experiences described by the participants in this study.

This study obtained knowledge as was created through the lived experiences of the participants. Insight into the experiences of participants was gained through interviews and data collection.

There are five important characteristics for a qualitative researcher to utilize: (a) natural setting, (b) description, (c) process, (d) inductive reasoning, and (e) meaning. A natural setting provides for an authentic environment with naturally occurring events. The natural setting and description provided context and explanatory accounts of the research topic which were preserved through: (a) including informal conversations, (b) extensive interviews, and (c) notes on the subject.

The inductive reasoning characteristic of qualitative research allowed for meaning to be derived from data collection and interviews without having established a hypothesis. The fifth feature that Bogdan and Biklen (1998) advise researchers to use in qualitative research is meaning. According to Lincoln and Denzin (1994), researchers should attempt to "make sense of or interpret phenomena in terms of the meanings people bring to them" (p. 2). Bogdan and Biklen (1998) cite Erickson (1986) and Dobbert (1982) as positing that:

> Meaning is of essential concern to the qualitative approach. Researchers
> are interested in how different people make sense of their lives. In
> other words, qualitative researchers are concerned with what are called
> participant perspectives (p. 7).

Given that the experiences of White faculty vary from one HBCU to the next, it was important to make sense of the varying ways in which White faculty developed perspectives about HBCUs. Phenomenological research allowed the researcher to discover the quintessence of White faculty experiences in their own words. The influx in numbers of White faculty at HBCUs is a phenomenon that was approached by analyzing the subjective observations of experiences as communicated by participants. According to Creswell (2003), phenomenology is both a philosophy and a method "to develop patterns and relationships of meaning" from extensive examination of a small sample group (p. 15).

ASSUMPTIONS AND BIASES

Relative to my subjective observations and experiences with White faculty at HBCUs from my perspectives as an HBCU student, HBCU alumnus, HBCU faculty member, HBCU staff member and former wife of a White HBCU faculty member, I expected to find that most White faculty were ignorant about the history and culture of HBCUs, in general, and their respective HBCUs, in particular, prior to employment. I expected that their perspectives and experiences as HBCU employees would be colored by their ignorance and historic socialization as privileged citizens in this country. Furthermore, I expected to find that in most cases where there was previous knowledge about HBCUs, it was approached as an ethnographic study with subconscious concepts of social Darwinism relative to the institution and its members.

As an HBCU graduate, there are two primary biases I have in relation to White faculty. The first primary bias is a question of the tendency of White faculty to be lenient with Black students to the point of debilitating the progress of some students compared to the practices of Black faculty on HBCU campuses. It often appears to me that this leniency is a result of low performance expectations for Black students by White faculty on HBCU campuses. The second primary bias I have is the observation of the relationship between numerous White faculty and Black students as one of novelty where the student serves as a case study or an amusing subject who might delight the White faculty member with tales from the other world as opposed to a student requiring serious guidance and professional engagement. Although not a primary bias, I hold that genuine White faculty knowledgeable of HBCU history with a non-judgmental perspective that respects the culture of HBCUs are a rarity.

When researchers interpret their participants' personal biographies, it is best to present biographical data in an objective manner. Ahern (1999) posited that although it is not "humanly possible" to exhibit total objectivity in one's research due to individual value systems, it is, however, "expected that researchers will make sincere efforts to put aside their values in order to more accurately describe respondents' life experiences" (p. 407). The researcher of the current study, intended to utilize reflexive bracketing to facilitate this process as well. According to Porter (1993) "[t]he advantage of this process is that the researcher's energies are spent more productively in trying to understand the effects of one's experience rather than engaging in futile attempts to eliminate them" (Ahern, 1999, p. 408).

For the sake of producing unbiased research, I "put aside personal feelings and preconception" (Ahern, 1999, p. 408). I kept a record of my perceptions of the participants' attitudes and tones in a reflexive journal. This journal also included various statements from the participants that I believed to be of importance. I hoped to minimize the possibility of presenting biases in my research by addressing my feelings that may cause a "lack of neutrality" (Ahern, 1999, p. 409). Bolstering my 'hope,' I had a committee of doctoral researchers and peer debriefers check my document for subjective terms and statements.

CONFIDENTIALITY

To protect the confidentiality of all information sources and as part of the agreement with the participants of the study and the Institutional Review Board for Human Subjects in Research at Jackson State University, each participant was asked to sign a consent form. The consent form included the nature and purpose of the study, a statement of voluntary participation, and protection of anonymity. In addition, pseudonym/ aliases were given to each participant and assigned to each institution for protection. Furthermore, personal information was concealed while in use and destroyed afterwards. Only the supervising faculty and researcher have access to the data collected.

SITE SELECTION

The two sites selected for this study, Ostin University (OU) and Rohan College (RC), were chosen primarily for their characteristics and their faculty composition, both analogous and dissimilar in scope. Ostin University is a large urban institution situated in the North and Rohan College is a small rural institution in the South. Both HBCUs are private not-for-profit, the latter having a religious affiliation.

Creswell (1998) asserts that "in a phenomenological study, the participants may be located at a single site, although they need not be" (p. 111). Consequently, I chose to utilize multiple participants from each institution for the purpose of obtaining various perspectives regarding their experiences within the respective HBCU where they were employed.

In order to ensure that a wide range of perspectives were incorporated into the study in terms of identifying White faculty perceptions at HBCUs, it was necessary to ascertain the classification of both institutions. Ostin University is an urban institution that is classified under Research Universities with high research activity (The Carnegie Foundation, 2006). As such, it offers a significant number of baccalaureate and graduate programs, awarding over 20 doctoral degrees annually- excluding the number of JD, MD, PharmD and other professional doctoral level degrees awarded each year. On the contrary, Rohan College is a rural institution which is classified under Baccalaureate Colleges – Diverse Fields (The Carnegie Foundation, 2006). Accordingly, this institution places major emphasis on its baccalaureate programs. In choosing these two institutions, I believed that I would reach a diverse group of participants with different perspectives on the racial climate. Generally, faculty at urban institutions are attracted to diverse surroundings where students originate from a range of backgrounds and the atmosphere is comparatively metropolitan. Equally are the faculty members diverse in terms of their backgrounds and experiences. On the other hand, rural faculty and students tend to be less diverse.

Site Profile: Ostin University (OU)

Ostin University, established in 1867, is a nonsectarian, private not-for-profit, four-year, high research activity HBCU located in a Mid-Atlantic urban city (The Carnegie Foundation, 2006). It has 12 schools within the university on 5 different campuses, and 10,623 students enrolled according to 2004 Carnegie Foundation data. The mean SAT score is above average and admission is competitive. Females comprise 65% and males 35% of the student population. In terms of the racial composition of the student body, 8,460 are Black, 199 are Asian or Pacific Islander, 114 are White or non-Hispanic, 80 Hispanic, 12 American Indian/ Alaska Native and 848 are unknown. Ostin University is home to 1,641 faculty of whom 41% are female and 59% are male. The distribution of degrees is 55% Doctorate, 26% First-professional, 16% Master's and 3% other; 83% of these degrees were earned from national research universities. Regarding faculty tenure, 580 are tenured, 199 tenure-track, 851 non-tenure track and 11 are other. The institution owns a television station and two radio stations, one of which ranks #1 in the city. The institution boasts the largest capital campaign in all of HBCU history. The university's core values maintain a commitment to diversity by establishing the institution as a place where African Americans and others can study free from hegemonic repression. Ostin University is dedicated to engendering a global community and equal opportunity for all.

Site Profile: Rohan College (RC)

Rohan College, established in 1905, is a sectarian, private not-for-profit, four-year, Baccalaureate College -- diverse fields HBCU (The Carnegie Foundation, 2006) located in a predominately Black Southern rural community. Student enrollment is 1,715, 55% female and 45% male. The racial/ethnic composition of the student body at RC is 1,670 Black non-

Hispanic, 10 White non-Hispanic and 31 unknown. Regarding faculty tenure status, according to 2007 data, 6 are tenured, 79 are tenure track and 9 are neither tenure nor tenure track. The institution offers undergraduate degrees through six academic divisions in 22 accredited baccalaureate degree programs. Rohan College launched its' first radio station in a neighboring rural community in 2009. The institutions' educational mission is intellectual, ethical, spiritual and service orientation for students in the context of a local community and global society.

Gaining Access

Creswell (2003) asserts the essential requirement for the researcher to establish a relationship with administrators of the institution who are able to provide necessary access to the researcher. I gained access to both HBCUs through the institutions' Vice President of Academic Affairs (VP). Hence, as the gatekeeper of the institution, the VP was responsible for providing me with the authorization that I needed to conduct the study. A letter (Appendix A) specifying the nature of my research, as well as a request for a list of faculty members of White descent, was sent via Email and U.S. Postal Service to the VP at each institution. Upon receipt of a letter of support and the list of White faculty members at each institution, I commenced the process of participant selection.

SAMPLE SELECTION

Sample criterion based selection was utilized to identify study participants and to meet basic criteria for quality assurance (Miles and Huberman, 1994). According to Creswell (1998) "criterion sampling is efficient for participants who have experienced a phenomenon" (p. 118). Since the study examined White faculty at HBCUs, the first criterion for this research was that participants must be White adults. Another criterion was that the participants be current White faculty members at the selected HBCUs. The final criterion was that the White faculty members be full-time, tenure-track employees at their respective HBCUs.

Access to names was requested from the appropriate campus authority. Upon acquiring these names, a structured process including telephones calls, email and written correspondence was utilized to recruit those individuals whose names were selected from the list at random. Specifically, I sent a letter via U.S. Postal Service and Email to all prospective participants on the list provided by the Office of Academic Affairs. The letter invited potential participants to participate in the study with criteria for inclusion noted in the letter. The invitation letter to all potential participants included information on the topic being explored as well as a request for their participation in the study. As indicated in the invitation letter, I contacted participants via telephone within one week of mailing the letters. This conversation confirmed receipt of the letter, requested their participation in the study and scheduled the time, date, and location of their interview for the study if they were willing to participate. Twelve participants (six per institution) were chosen to participate in this study. Subsequent to the follow-up telephone call, I sent a letter of agreement via U.S. Postal Service and Email thanking each participant for agreeing to participate. This confirmation letter also included confirmation of the date, time, and meeting place for the interview. In addition, the consent form was included with the confirmation letter for participants to review prior to the scheduled interview. In order to reassure all participants of their security, the consent form provided detailed information regarding the disposal of the data following the completion of the study. Approximately two days before the scheduled interview, I contacted each participant by telephone to remind him/her of our appointment and then again via Email.

INTERVIEWS

Interviews are an interactional communication process between two individuals where at least one has a predetermined purpose. Interviewing involves asking and answering questions. Researchers can recover valuable information from participants via the interview process. Researchers conducting phenomenological studies primarily collect data via in-depth interviews.

I gathered an adequate interpretation of the participants' perceptions through both nonverbal and verbal modes of communication, such as body language and tone of voice in addition to their personal narratives. Fundamentally, the utilization of an interview guide was a vital component of conducting a well-organized interview.

The interview guide for this study was created to assist the researcher during the interview process. In order to remain focused on the topic, guides were designed for the interviews. It was critical that the interview questions be constructed in order to facilitate addressing the research questions for this study.

The themes and subject areas explored in the interview for this study surrounded issues that contributed to addressing the research questions for this study. Such issues included perceptions of HBCUs prior to employment, faculty-student and professional relationships, as well as institutional values. In addition, it was also necessary for the interview questions to explore White faculty perceptions of diversity at their respective institution.

Researchers can develop insight on participant's perceptions by gathering descriptive data as communicated by participants. Furthermore, according to Stewart and Cash (2006), a researcher will benefit by examining the topic for conversation in advance in order to "reveal past attitudes and opinions and speculations about current attitudes and opinions," thereby providing insights into "the nature and size of the population" to be sampled and "the complexities of the issue" (p. 126).

Interviews were scheduled for durations of one hour to provide adequate time for participants requiring more time. The interviews were conducted in the following manner:

Consent. Participants were given consent forms prior to the interview. Upon review, they were asked if any concerns existed that were not addressed. The participants signed two forms, one for the researcher and one for their personal file. Likewise, participants were given the opportunity to ask questions and voice their concerns upon satisfactory completion of the interview.

Opening. The tape recorder was started. An introduction of the researcher from a script written in advance was given, followed by a review of the purpose for both the interview and the study. The first questions explored demographic information, followed by those relating directly to the research.

Closing. The participant was asked if s/he would like to readdress any of the questions. An explanation of how the data will be utilized followed. Finally, the researcher expressed appreciation for the participant's time and effort and then turned off the tape recorder.

DATA COLLECTION

In-depth interviewing is a key mode of data collection in qualitative research. Interviewing is a conversation with purpose. In particular, phenomenological interviewing will be utilized. The process of phenomenological interviewing is comprised of three steps which include: a focus on past experiences, a focus on present experiences and a subsequent combination of these experience to describe the individual's overall experience with the phenomenon.

Phenomenological reduction is the next phase of phenomenological interviewing. At this phase, data are organized by themes. Structural synthesis is the final stage and involves the exploration of "all possible meanings and divergent perspectives" (Creswell, 1998, p. 150).

The advantage of this interviewing process is that it allowed for the interspersing of the researcher's perspective with that of the participant. Additionally, field notes were taken as part of the researcher's observation of the participant and the environment.

Field Notes

Subsequent to observations or interviews the researcher prepared field notes. Within these notes, the researcher renders a description of people, objects, places, events, activities and conversations. There are two types of data which materialize from a researcher's field notes. The first is description and the other form is reflection. The researcher's description notes comprised a detailed summation of observations. The description encapsulated: (1) portraits of the subject; (2) reconstruction of dialogue; (3) description of physical setting; (4) accounts of particular events; (5) depiction of activities; and (6) the observer's behavior. The identification of such data provided the researcher with a true depiction of the occurrences taking place throughout the study. Conversely, reflective field notes underscored the researcher's speculations, feelings, problems, ideas, hunches, impressions, and prejudices.

Transcribing

Transcribing data refers to the process of listening to tape recorded interviews or observations and writing down what is heard verbatim. For the purpose of this study each interview was transcribed verbatim according to the guidelines established by Bogdan and Biklen (1998).

Data Analysis

The researcher tape recorded, transcribed and examined interview transcripts and field notes gathered from meetings with the selected White faculty at the chosen HBCUs according to strategies outlined by Marshall and Rossman (2006). These data were coded into categories by pertinent words and phrases. The study followed the six typical analytical procedures according to Marshall and Rossman (2006): (a) organizing data; (b) generating categories, themes and patterns; (c) coding the data; (d) testing initial understandings; (e.) searching for alternative explanations; and (f) writing the report.

Coding

Bogdan and Biklen (1998) maintain that "[d]eveloping a list of coding categories after the data have been collected" is "a crucial step in data analysis" (p. 171). Miles and Huberman (1994) define the process as the compilation of various abstract pieces of data into homogeneous groups that are then attached to a code that might be tied to a specific theme. The utilization of thematic codes was necessary to organize and record recurring patterns throughout the field notes and transcripts. As such, data and themes were identified and cross-referenced by the doctoral research committee. Subsequent to collapsing and redefining the themes, the transcripts were reexamined to make certain that all emergent themes were identified.

Trustworthiness

Lincoln and Guba (1985) suggest determining the "worth" of a researcher's queries and findings through the evaluation of four facets: credibility, transferability, dependability and confirmability. Credibility was established through honest presentation of data collected from participants. Transferability refers to the capacity for the data collected to be utilized for other forms of research. Dependability refers to the efficiency of data analysis and evaluation. Lastly, confirmability is the extent to which the data collected supports findings.

In order to ensure credibility, I conducted interviews with participants who have experienced the phenomenon. I also asked participants to clarify any lingering questions before commencing data analysis. Moreover, all field notes were reviewed and reflected on in a journal. Within the journal, I kept track of my perceptions of the participants' attitudes and tones. This journal also included various statements from the participants that I believed to be of importance.

Regarding transferability of this study, I presented the findings in a manner which allowed the reader to determine applicability to context. Thus, the reader of this study should be able to make the connection between his/her own context and the current study by acknowledging both the specifics of the individuals involved in the study as well as the circumstances surrounding the topic of the study.

The research of a dependable study will last over time and will add depth to future research studies. Dependability also ensures that all sectors of the study are truthful. Researchers should incorporate a trail that is auditable to ensure dependability. Hence, in order to ensure that the current study is dependable, the researcher incorporated day-to-day occurrences, a personal log of events, methodological transformations, and notes on the researcher's intellectual evolvement in relation to the study. This will assist the others in confirming the study's level of dependability.

Furthermore, a researcher should establish confirmability when conducting a study. This facet of trustworthiness is identified as incorporating a level of objectivity. The researcher of this study established confirmability in the same manner that dependability is established, through an audit trail. This provided verification of the process undertaken by the researcher. This process emphasized the data collection process in the interpretations to be made by the researcher.

DELIMITATIONS/LIMITATIONS

The delimitations of this study included the singular implementation of qualitative methods and a focus on only full-time, tenure-line White faculty from two HBCUs. Furthermore, the limitations of the study included utilization of a sample of White faculty making it difficult to generalize the findings; however, the varying HBCU characteristics helped to provide balance. Another limitation was the possibility that fear for their professional livelihood might have impeded the willingness of White faculty to respond to interview questions without reservation or to even participate at all; however, this was countered by written assurance to the participant of confidentiality. Finally, the race of the researcher may have served as a limitation in conducting interviews with White faculty who might have felt uncomfortable answering questions concerning race in said presence. However, as much as possible, a rapport was developed in advance of beginning the interview in order to counter any insecurities.

There are those who talk, and without knowledge or forethought
reveal a truth which they themselves do not understand.
And there are those who have the truth within them,
but they tell it not in words.

KAHLIL GIBRAN
on 'Talking' from *The Prophet* (1923)

7 WHITE FACULTY PERSPECTIVES ILLUMINATED

FINDINGS

The principal objective of this study was to explore the behavioral and psychological experiences of White faculty at Historically Black Colleges and Universities (HBCUs). Specifically, this investigation focused on the racial climate at HBCUs as perceived by White Faculty. A close analysis of participants' collective experiences revealed themes that correlated directly to the conceptual framework. In particular, the four dimensions of racial climate were evidenced in the statements conveyed by participants. Principally, the structural diversity of HBCUs was found to be in harmony with the historical legacy of inclusion at historically Black institutions. Furthermore, the historical legacy of inclusion and structural diversity generated overwhelmingly positive experiences among participants relative to the behavioral and psychological dimensions of campus climate at HBCUs.

This chapter is divided into four sections. The first section provides a description of the institution sites. Detailed information regarding the participants in this study, specifically their education, length of employment at their respective HBCU and previous experiences, are presented in the second section. The third section presents common themes as they relate to the research questions and illustrates participants' experiences as they correlate directly to the Four Dimensions of Campus Climate framework. The final section explores themes that do not address the research questions of this study, although they emerged during data analysis as significantly laudable topics that may plausibly advance the comprehension of racial climate as perceived by White faculty at HBCUs.

DESCRIPTION OF SITES

Two four-year institutions were selected as sites for this study. The selected sites were identified as Ostin University (OU) and Rohan College (RC). Ostin University, located in an urban area, is classified as a nonsectarian, private not-for-profit, four-year, high research activity HBCU. Rohan College (RC), located in a rural locale, is a sectarian, private not-for-profit, four-year, baccalaureate college -- diverse fields HBCU.

Ostin University, situated in the center of a major urban city, was established by and with congressional appropriations shortly after the issuance of the last of President Abraham Lincoln's post-Civil War proclamations, to educate men and women of all races. OU is home to one of the world's largest and most comprehensive repositories on the African Diaspora- African and their descendants around the world, predominately in the Americas, Europe and the Middle East. OU has been home to the first Black Rhodes Scholar and Nobel Peace Prize Winner. OU was the intellectual force behind the Harlem Renaissance, nurturer to the person who coined the term "Black Power," and the springing board for the individual who would argue and win Brown v. Board of Education and go on to become the first Black Supreme Court Justice. Among other OU alumni are several prominent Black female and male politicians, novelists, scientists, musicians, historians and actors. Several of the first Greek sororities and fraternal organizations were founded at OU. The institution is a publisher and producer of several major academic journals. OU has the largest endowment of any HBCUs and even ranks above numerous HWIs. The main campus sits on 258 acres with 115 buildings with another 22 acre and 108 acre campus in addition to another smaller campus and facility operations building in the city. The main campus still maintains several of its historic buildings including the building which housed its founding agency. OU does, however, have newer edifices- some as recent as the 21st century.

Rohan College, is a sectarian, four-year liberal arts, historically Black institution situated on over 50 acres of land in a rural, yet comparatively populated sector of town. RC was established by a religious denomination in a Confederate State to serve African American students. The institution has an open admissions policy and is the fastest growing amongst smaller HBCUs. It enrolls students primarily from its home state. The quaint campus has served as a safe-haven and meeting place for actors in the Civil Rights Movement. Rohan College has grown from the 10 acre campus acquired by its founders to being positioned on over 50 acres of land with a recently purchased adjacent campus of 25 acres. It maintains 16 buildings, among them a restored historic administration building. RC has a highly ranked marching band and is supported by a strong alumni base and surrounding community.

DESCRIPTION OF SAMPLE

For this study, twelve faculty members, six per institution, were selected to participate. Of the twelve participants, four were females and eight were males. As such, faculty members represented various disciplines. Coincidently, each participant in the study earned his/her doctorate from an accredited historically White institution of higher education in the United States. Tables 1 and 2 provide pseudonyms for the faculty members who participated in the study at Ostin University and Rohan College, respectively. Each table is followed by an annotated narrative that introduces the participants and a first-person account provides information on their background and experience.

Ostin University

Table 1
Participants at Ostin University (OU)

NAME	GENDER	YEARS AT OSTIN UNIVERSITY	PREVIOUS HBCU	PREVIOUS HWI
Ben	Male	40 yrs	n/a	X
Joan	Female	24 yrs	n/a	X
Drew	Male	28 yrs	n/a	X
Lindsay	Female	15 yrs	n/a	X
Ellen	Female	12 yrs	X	n/a
Floyd	Male	8 yrs	n/a	X

Six faculty members were interviewed at OU. Five were tenured (two males and three females) and one male was on the tenure-track. Most of the faculty members who were interviewed at OU had been teaching at the institution for over 20 years. Faculty members at OU who chose to be interviewed for this study were assigned a pseudonym. Thus, it is appropriate to introduce each participant.

Ben, a tenured professor and ranking administrator at OU, has been employed at the institution for 40 years. He admits to having earned his degrees from "elite" HWIs. Ben taught briefly at an HWI, as a graduate student; however, OU was his first HBCU. Thinking back over four decades, Ben recalls his initial decision to work with Ostin University as follows:

> I was a graduate student at [name withheld] and a professor here
> knew a professor there, and he was looking for a couple of people
> who had linguistic training who could work on a research project
> that he had... I don't remember thinking about it a whole lot. I
> wasn't very conscious. I don't remember being particularly
> conscious of [Ostin University] being an HBCU... It was just a job
> and I was going to work for a particular person. I wasn't going to
> be involved with students in particular I was just going to have a
> job over there. Over here at [Ostin]. So, I came, and I got started;
> my primary reason really had nothing to do with it being an
> HBCU. It had to do with my wanting a job and my scholarship
> had run out. [Ostin] was really to be a research assistant. My
> fellowship I had had at [name withheld] had run out and so I
> needed something. It didn't pay much. It paid four thousand five
> hundred dollars I think. So, then I was working as a research
> assistant for a man who was actually Indian from India. I worked
> for him, and I did research for him. I met students in passing. I
> met a few graduate students but I really wasn't particularly focused
> on it being an HBCU.

Currently, Ben is both a tenured professor and an Assistant Dean. He studies African culture and is in the midst of an extensive African language project. He has lived in Africa and belongs to an African American male support group. Since his employment at OU he has had serious intimate relationships with an African and an African American woman. He enjoys intimate conversations with his African students in their native languages of which he is knowledgeable and embraces his personal relationships with African American students who frequent his office for advice and laughs.

Ben is godfather to an Ethiopian boy and often hosts African families visiting the United States at his private residence.

Joan had taught at four prominent HWIs before assuming a faculty position at Ostin University. In the 24 years that she has worked at OU she has been a faculty member and Department Chair. In that time, she also earned tenure. She explained her reason for assuming a position at OU:

> I was in administration at the [name withheld] and I wanted to get
> back to teaching. They wanted someone to come and develop
> their public relations program.

Joan, grew-up a self-proclaimed "army-brat," having lived all over the world in a variety of cultures and among a mixture of races and ethnicities. Although she believes that her early exposure to diversity prepared her to live in a global society and work at OU, Joan discovered upon assuming her position that she still had a lot to learn.

> I had lived in North Africa as a child; my father was military. I
> moved around a lot, so diversity was just sort of every day to me. I
> didn't really see color so much but when I came to [Ostin] there
> was a lot that I learned about some of the issues that African
> Americans have about their skin and the different colors. I
> thought black was black. I didn't know that there were lots of
> different shades of black. Even when you think that you are
> comfortable in an environment, you still have a lot to learn about
> that diverse environment.

Drew has been with OU for 28 years and has earned tenure. He had worked at an HWI but never at an HBCU. He is very direct and describes himself as "quirky." He says about his reason for assuming a position with OU:

> I was relocating to the [name withheld] from my hometown. I
> applied to every university in the area and [Ostin University] was
> the only institution to offer me an interview and a position.

Lindsay earned her doctorate from a high research activity HWI. She has tenure with Ostin University and has worked there for 15 years. She had never been employed at an HBCU but applied to OU when she and her husband moved to the area. Lindsay had heard of OU before and was "excited" to learn about an available position. She was not "deterred" from submitting her vitae for consideration by only having had prior experience working with an HWI. Admitting that her prior knowledge about OU had largely to do with its "reputation as a good Black university," Lindsay thought working at an HBCU, OU in particular, would be a "fun and refreshing experience."

Ellen is a tenured professor at Ostin University. She initially became interested in OU when conducting research. Ellen saw OU as a place where she could develop her research further and enthusiastically accepted when she was offered a position at the university. Like Lindsay, Ellen viewed OU as a prestigious institution among HBCUs. However unlike Lindsay, Ellen had previously worked for an HBCU but not an HWI. She has been at OU for 12 years.

Floyd is on the tenure-track at Ostin University. He worked at two HWIs before seeking employment at OU. While he had never worked at an HBCU, he considers himself familiar with the "campus culture" due to the number of "personal friends" he has who attended HBCUs. Floyd reminisced that on a few occasions he attended parties at an HBCU near his undergraduate institution with a friend and often wondered what academic life resembled.

> I was always complaining about my job at [name withheld]. I never really fit in. It never felt right to me. I know that sounds kind of weird. Anyway, I used to come over here a lot to have lunch with a friend of mine over in the Communications Department. So, he works here. He said he would stay on the lookout for an opening and the rest is history. Here I am. I know a lot of people and I had a few choices of places to go, places to work.

Floyd has been at OU for 8 years and prides himself on "understanding" the culture at OU. He believes that because of his early experiences he can "make people feel more comfortable" around him.

Rohan College

Table 2
Participants at Rohan College (RC)

NAME	GENDER	YEARS AT ROHAN COLLEGE	PREVIOUS HBCU	PREVIOUS HWI
Patrick	Male	6 yrs	n/a	X
Cindy	Female	4 yrs	n/a	X
Bob	Male	30 yrs	n/a	X
Davis	Male	18 yrs	n/a	n/a
John	Male	6 yrs	n/a	X
Brad	Male	10 yrs	n/a	X

Six faculty members were interviewed at Rohan College. Rohan College has only 12 tenured faculty at the institution; none of those interviewed were tenured. Each of the six faculty members interviewed were tenure-track (one female and five males). Half of the faculty members who were interviewed at RC had been teaching at the institution for less than 10 years. Faculty members at RC who chose to be interviewed for this study were assigned a pseudonym. Thus, it is appropriate to introduce each participant.

Patrick came to the institution after working at three different HWIs, two public and one private. He has been at Rohan College for six years and declared his primary reason for accepting a position at the institution as: "I needed a job. I mean that was really a primary reason for accepting."

Patrick was born in the South and has spent his professional career, thus far, in the South. He plans someday to move to a rural part of Northern California where he hopes to work as an administrator. Despite his previous marriage to a woman from which two children were born, Patrick is now openly gay. He believes that the state of California and its institutions would feel more relaxed and be more tolerant of his interracial same-sex marriage with a Black man.

Cindy believes that her reason for being at Rohan College is a matter of "Divine" order. She says, "I just felt that very suddenly God had opened that door for me." Cindy worked at three HWIs for a total of over 12 years before coming to RC where she has now been for 4 years. She continues to work part-time for a public historically White university located several miles from RC in the state's largest city.

Bob's relationship with RC "goes back about 30 years," and he feels his perceptions are "different" for this reason. He worked extensively with HWIs throughout his professional career and came to RC as a "favor." Bob admitted to his discomfort with a structured interview alluding to his preference to direct the conversation as he discussed his background and reason for coming to Rohan College.

> I interview a little differently. I mean we can do the interview but
> let me give you my background first. I taught at the University of
> [withheld] and [withheld] University back before I came to
> [university acronym withheld], and I taught at [university acronym
> withheld]. I came to [university acronym withheld] in 1977, retired
> from there after 25 years. So, my first year here, was the latter part
> of the year into the second year, so that would make it '78, '79.
> [Rohan] College was deteriorating very badly and I think it was
> down to 400 or so students. The campus physically was in bad
> shape and they asked for people to try and come over and support
> some of the endeavors here, teach, or whatever we could from

[university acronym withheld]. I think there were only two of us maybe, but I was one of those two people. So my relationship to [Rohan] College goes back about 30 years. It goes back that far, and maybe I answer with a different perception than somebody who just was hired here in the last 3 or 4 years. Then, of course Dr. [name withheld] came who was just, to me, the best president I'd ever worked for and I've worked for a lot of great presidents. You know? I mean I couldn't think more of somebody than [president's name withheld- HWI], and [president's name withheld-HWI] but [former RC president] was just fabulous and what he did was tremendous and I feel the same way about [current president of RC]. I was just thankful that they hired him. I know that is who [former RC president] wanted and how can you beat that? The person who rebuilt it you better respect who he thinks is ready. So my perception is a little bit different to these questions, okay? I forget how many years ago, it must have been about five years now maybe four; RC had somebody leave them in September in the division of education. So they called [name withheld] and [name withheld] called me, a friend of mine, and so I talked to [name withheld] and I came on in September of that year and taught for the full year. I came and taught for [RC] because with that person having left [the division] so suddenly left them kind of in the lurch and it also endangered their accreditation based on the fact of diversity of faculty etcetera. The [department head] said to me they were trying to get NCATE accreditation, which is nice, plus credentials for the education division. [NCATE] is nationally recognized and [Rohan College] had never had it. The [department head] is kind of an expert in [NCATE accreditation] and that is something that she really wanted to do. So she called me and we talked about me teaching a course and basically it was because they needed a diverse faculty member in the division of education.

Davis had never worked at an HWI or an HBCU prior to commencing employment at Rohan College almost 18 years ago. Davis earned a juris doctorate from the law school at RC in 1993. When asked whether there were other white students in his class he responded: "There were at the time but none that graduated with me. There would be a number of White graduates that would come behind my class."

For Davis, his career at Rohan College, now spanning nearly two decades, began with an "ask," from a ranking administrator who had knowledge of his extensive work in his specialization, and thereby, sought to employ his expertise for the benefit of the college and its students,

> At the time the area was in Communications on the academic side. The reason for taking the position was simply because it started out as an ask on behalf of the then academic dean who knew of my experience within television and asked that I would come and help with the reorganization of the communications program. The guy who was over the program had gotten very ill, and shortly after I had come on board died. After his death, I was asked to come on full-time to take control or to give some guidance to the area. And that's how I got here.

Taking full advantage of the tuition reimbursement extended to faculty for children and spouses, Davis enrolled his oldest daughter at Rohan College in 2003. His daughter was active on the volleyball team for the two years she attended RC. She then enrolled at a state HWI where she graduated 3 years later.

John earned a doctorate in math from a state HWI. He knew very little about HBCUs in general and RC in particular. He accepted a position at RC after working one year at another state HWI simply, "because they offered me the job." John has been employed at Rohan College for six years and travels nearly four hours to and from the suburb where he lives to work each day at the institution.

Brad has been employed at Rohan College since 1999, ten years. He had never before worked at an HBCU. Brad earned his doctorate from a state HWI, where he also worked. He then assumed a position at another public HWI upon graduation. He considers himself a "liberal-democrat" and had first come to teach at RC as a "favor." In a detailed first-person account, Brad shared the events in his professional and personal life leading up to his primary reason for accepting a position at RC,

> The primary reason was, that at the time I was working in retail. We had our own business, like a music store. We had music, books… and I went ahead and got a certification to teach. I thought I might want to teach but I'm not sure, the retail thing was going so well. I was involved in the thing at [name of neighborhood withheld], the whole movement, like when they revitalized [name of neighborhood withheld] and it was so exciting and people were doing so well- this was so long back this was in '77. I thought, I have my doctorate and a certification and someday I really will teach but I'll do this for a while. [The

music/book business] became like a career… after I'd done that, for about 10 or 15 years I was asked to teach some American Lit classes at [name of HWI withheld] which I started doing part-time. That's what kind of got me back into the profession and then of course one day the phone rings. I think it was one of those kind of situations where somebody was [at RC] and they were in the middle of class and something happened. The Chairperson of the Humanities Division knew I was out there and that I was teaching English and I was doing a really good job and so I got the call just out of nowhere. I was like okay I guess I can do this but only if you are desperate because it was only to fill in. I said, 'I'll do this as a favor.' I got over [to RC] and I did that as a substitute… part-time for a semester. I really started to enjoy it, it was different than teaching at [name of HWI withheld] which was what I was doing and [name of HWI withheld] for a year. I like it better for me some reason, I think it may be ideological. I have lived in the inner-city; I grew up in a suburb but vowed that once I left the suburbs I would never return. I like sidewalks and people from all over the world and… I've just always been fascinated by people who from, people who are different. And so when I came [to RC] I felt like, wow I really like this.

FINDINGS PRESENTED USING APPROPRIATE ANALYSIS TECHNIQUES
PERCEPTIONS OF RACIAL CLIMATE

In my analysis of the interviews with participants at both OU and RC, I discovered information that provided insight into the perceptions that White faculty may have of racial climate on HBCU campuses. An analysis of the data resulted in the emergence of themes that were common to faculty at both institutions. As such, it was revealed that White faculty members surmised among primary factors influencing their perceptions of racial climate were organizational culture and faculty/ student interactions. White faculty members in this study articulated a transformation in their views about historically Black institutions. The absence of overt diversity initiatives was noted as was the nonexistence of institutional objectives to develop a diverse faculty. Based on the themes of the campus climate framework, a portrait of White faculty perceptions of racial climate at two HBCUs is presented.

HISTORICAL LEGACY OF INCLUSION

Historically Black Colleges and Universities were established after emancipation to educate Blacks who were constitutionally denied academic instruction; consequently there were few trained Black teachers. Thus, White faculty initially served as the primary educators at these institutions. Hence, HBCUs have a documented historical legacy of inclusion from their establishment for Blacks by the financial, political and intellectual contributions of White missionaries and sometimes government agencies. Traditionally, these institutions have, without exception, been welcome to faculty and student of all nationalities, races, religions and genders. Findings in this study revealed that even today HBCUs sustain a historical legacy of inclusion.

Bob, who has been with RC for 30 years, says that one of the things he likes about the institution is how "close" the faculty is to him, "I mean they just treat me like family and we treat each other, I think, that way." Comparatively speaking, he continues:

> I didn't experience that, at [HWI]. They were great to me and
> being on merit pay was the best thing that ever happened to me
> because I made a bunch of money doing it… But, it was also an
> institution where there was a lot of, to use a common vernacular,
> backstabbing. Jealousy.

Davis believes that HBCUs have always been "inviting," and from extensive research on RC in particular states:

> I've done research on this particular institution. There has always
> been a very diverse and internationally diverse faculty. We've had
> individuals that have come from as far away as Nigeria, Japan,
> China, Korea, and even Italy. We've had people from there and
> the diversity continues.

Brad "loves" working at RC where he "felt immediately" a sense of belonging as compared to [HWI] where it was "hard" for him.

> I don't think predominately White institutions have a clue. I don't
> think they have any idea about what's going on outside of their
> little privileged lifestyles. I've become a more holistic teacher since
> I've been here.

Interestingly, although faculty at Ostin University articulate an air of inclusion at the institution, personal feelings of "carefulness" and not being an "insider" persist. Ben has been at Ostin University 40 years.

I've watched a lot of new people come and I came through myself.
I think that there is kind of a background that this is an HBCU so
Blackness is part of this university.

Still he feels that White faculty members "are pretty much equally
involved in embracing what [Ostin University] is." Nevertheless, aware of
"Blackness" at OU, Davis expresses apprehension on the part of White
faculty regarding inclusion.

I think race is kind of there all of the time. So, I think that
sometimes White faculty might be a little slow to feel totally loyal.
I think they don't become insiders.

Notwithstanding, he maintains that:

The Black community is generally more sensitive to being receptive
of difference because it's kind of a principle because they've been
hurt themselves. So many people have been hurt themselves by
being rejected by others. I think that many Black community
members are readier to be accepting of diversity and I think that
White institutions, [HWIs] could learn from them.

Likewise, Lindsay observes an "open" and "fair" atmosphere at HBCUs
and OU in particular; yet, she put across her own feelings of "an unspoken
attitude of seeing if you're going to fit in." She could not describe the
"behaviors" that caused her this feeling but maintained, "I have felt that.
Just a little bit of caution from others until they saw if I could fit or not."
Acknowledging her self-prescribed apprehension, Lindsay admitted that
"no one ever said that."

Lindsay feels that "people take care of each other" at OU and a "sense
of active community" unlike at a PWI. Still she feels outside of this
phenomenon, confiding in the researcher:

Just me being in this environment, I carry such a sense of
carefulness. There is an awareness that there is a difference and I
want to be careful with that.

Pondering whether her feelings are "a common characteristic when in a
minor situation," Lindsay disclosed her feelings about exclusivity at an HWI
where she worked previously:

I felt that way when I was a minority by gender and I was careful
about the perception I was setting. I was very careful when we
would have faculty meetings… I was very careful to make sure that
I was never the one to make coffee. That was the kind of

carefulness about gender but I don't carry carefulness about gender here, but I do carry carefulness about race.

STRUCTURAL DIVERSITY

A 2001 NCES data report on HBCUs reveals a total of 178 White faculty at the two sites in this study. Other faculty comprised 350 members of the faculty across campuses. Black faculty represented 786 of the faculty at these institutions.

Specifically, the racial composition of faculty at the private, research university located in an urban city was 742 Black, 161 White and 345 Other. The small, private college, located in a rural area, reported a faculty that included 44 Black, 17 White and 5 Other faculty members.

Ellen believes that there are vast reasons for faculty seeking employment at an HBCU:

> Faculty choose to work at HBCUs for so many reasons. I imagine
> that many African Americans have connections to HBCUs like
> family or they graduated from the institution or maybe they want to
> work within their community. Most White faculty I think come
> here for professional reasons like research or location or needing
> employment or reputation in their discipline, something like that.

However varied the reasons may be, per Ellen, for faculty seeking employment at an HBCU, the numbers indicate a wide stratification of faculty by racial composition at the two sites in this study.

PSYCHOLOGICAL DIMENSION

The psychological dimension of racial climate addressed diversity, perceptions of discrimination, group relations and attitudes toward those of other ethnic groups. Participants were unanimous in some respects while they diverged widely in their opinions and experiences on other accounts, as evidenced in the following section.

Diversity

Participants unanimously voiced the opinion that diversity was of great significance. Accordingly, seven of the participants indicated that having a diverse faculty was an intentional objective of the institution. Joan (OU) said,

> I think that is has become increasingly important to leadership on
> this campus because [OU] touts itself as an international university.

We have students from over 130 foreign countries attending the
university and just about every state in the United States. It is
important for a lot of reasons…

Ben reflected on his 40 years at OU as he expressed his thoughts on the
significance of having a diverse faculty.

I find for myself, my being at [Ostin University] for all these years
has certainly enriched my own life. I think it's become an
experience that has forced me or allowed me to understand
diversity in America and to understand diversity in this country in a
way that I never would have understood without ever having been
at [OstinUniversity.] So I think it deepens my own experience. It
opens new doors for me academically because I find lots of
examples that challenge me that have to do with the Black
experience in America. When I'm talking about language and
linguistics I wind up getting involved with attitudes towards Black
English and things like that. So, I think it makes the experience a
lot richer and it prepares all of us for living in a world which is a
global community.

Although Ben thinks being a part of a diverse faculty is important, Joan
does not think the racial distribution of faculty at an institution is a
determining factor for students during the college selection process.

I don't know that students really think about it. I guess it depends
on the level. At the undergraduate level, they don't have a clue.
They look at the institution and they look at the parties. I don't
think when students are picking an undergraduate program that
they even know what the faculty is like. I've had students come to
OU and they were from predominately White high schools and
they were in culture shock because there were so many Black
faculty, and I've had students come from predominately Black high
schools and they came here and they were stunned that there was
such a diverse faculty that they had Asian faculty, Hispanic faculty.
So, I don't think that it is something that they think about. I think
that at the graduate level when students are looking to study
something in a particular discipline they are more aware of who is
there and what their area of expertise is but not necessarily the
color of their skin or their ethnic background I don't think it is a
reason that they choose to come to a campus.

Joan believes that faculty may be only slightly more concerned about diversity at an institution.

> I think there are some faculty who only want to work at HBCUs. Again because of the historic nature of HBCUs, they have a commitment and they want to. We have faculty who come here and they can't wait to get out fast enough to go back to a state university or community college. You know I think it's an individual call.

Five faculty members responded that diversifying the faculty at their respective institution was not a premeditated objective. Among those faculty, several stated "maybe", "I'm not sure" or "not really" before delivering a definitive negative response. Cindy was among the latter:

> Not really. From my first experience as full-time faculty I know that comments were made about the fact that the Humanities Division is kind of the White division because we have, more, a greater percent I think of White faculty, or non-Black because we do have an Asian on the staff. The concern seemed to be that there is too much diversity in our division. But I think, it just happened, it wasn't planned or intentional.

Bob used advertisements for prospective faculty members to make his point about diversity not being an intentional objective of the institution.

> I'm not so sure it is an intentional objective because when I see a faculty position open, when I see a chair person looking for faculty members, I think for the most part they advertise and the advertisement is not saying that we are looking for a Black professor a White professor or any kind of professor. I think they are looking for a competent professor with certain academic achievements. So, really, I don't think it is an objective of the institution.

Related to the importance of diversity, participants were asked about the topic of diversity during the interview, at orientation, or at faculty development workshops. Interestingly, ten participants did not recall any dialogue on diversity during workshops, training or initial meetings. Only, two participants responded positively. Bob was in the minority having remembered that during his interview the topic of diversity was addressed and he added that, "it was handled so professionally." Patrick also felt that the topic of diversity was addressed.

> They mentioned that we would be dealing with a lot of first
> generation college students. That was the main emphasis. I think
> they mentioned the fact that this is an HBCU and that they also
> had an open door policy. That was mentioned and that they may
> have a variety of socio-economic backgrounds.

Joan explicitly remembered the type of training received at OU and courses that broached the topic of diversity.

> We've not had diversity training, as such. We've had sexual
> harassment training and we have had courses through our
> leadership academy about the history of the institution. Learning
> about the history of the institution tends to touch the issues of
> diversity as the historical reason for the institution to be founded.
> In terms of having special workshops at the time, no. Now, there
> are a couple of courses that are taught at our Center for Excellence
> in Teaching Learning and Assessments on dealing with a diverse
> classroom. They are optional courses; they are not required.

Perceptions of Discrimination

Only two faculty of twelve participants perceived any racial discrimination at their respective HBCU. Interestingly, both faculty members reporting incidences of racial tension were employed at the small, rural Rohan College. Patrick conveyed a sense of frustration as he recalled his condemnation by peers for advocating on behalf of a student with dyslexia,

> There was racial conflict several years back in dealing with a
> student with disabilities. I mean learning disabilities. I had a
> student who was severely dyslexic and he could neither read nor
> write anything, and the student was Black. Myself and another
> colleague advocated for him mainly because we had understandings
> of learning disabilities- I taught exceptional education on the high
> school level. Comments were made from others on campus that
> they didn't understand why we had such an interest in a Black
> student since we weren't Black. It had nothing to do with the racial
> identity of anyone. It had mainly to do with advocating for a
> student with a disability in an institution that openly said it would

60

not provide for that student although there were legal requirements to do so.

Similarly, John experienced racial tension at Rohan College but not from colleagues. Early in his career, he encountered discomfort when a guest orator at the college's Honor's Convocation spoke critically of Whites. John recalled amusingly:

> The only time that I had an issue was... I think it was my first year here, maybe my second. There was an honors convocation and the speaker started- it seemed to me- denigrating Whites as a group, all of them. I'm just sitting there going, 'Okay, and I'm listening to this 'cause why?' I think that's the only time that I have had any issue that I am aware of. I may have caused issues that I didn't realize. That's the only thing that I've noticed and that was early on. Maybe I just got less sensitive or more sensitive and haven't noticed that since.

Interestingly, two participants at the large, urban Ostin University spoke of racial incidents that were not directed at them personally. Specifically, Joan observed preferential treatment of White faculty by Black faculty while they discriminated toward each other.

> I will be brutally frank in some of the things I've observed. I think we have a very collegial faculty but I think sometimes White faculty are treated better than African American faculty by African Americans. I never understood, I mean I always knew there was a class system. Sometimes I will observe that I've been on committees with people that will treat me very cordially and give me opportunities that they might not give to their African American colleague or might not treat their African American colleague as well. Sometimes it is simply a matter of the way you talk to them, the vernacular that you might use.

Despite the fact that Ellen had not perceived any discrimination directed against her, she described offensive behavior that she had observed from students.

I haven't felt or I don't think I have felt discriminated against. No. Students make comments under their breath sometimes but students will say things when they're angry. I am even surprised that students will say the N-word within earshot. That's more offensive than anything I ever heard them mumble about me.

While neither of these racial incidents was directed toward the participants, the behavior of the individuals was viewed negatively or offensively.

Three participants were prudent about their assessment of perceived discrimination or racism, disclosing that the issue is oftentimes problematical. Ben has contemplated whether discrimination or race might play a role in the process of promotion.

> There is almost nothing there. What does come to mind is if I had had ambitions to become Dean or a higher administrator I have a sense that *not* being Black might have played a role there, but even as I say that I'm thinking about the Associate Provost who is a White guy. He was chosen because he is a good competent guy. So I have a little bit of sense that promotion to higher levels of administration and possibly even academic promotion could be affected by race. But my own is that there has been no problem for me and I just don't think about it very much.

Drew feels it is sometimes difficult to discern discrimination or racism.

> Sometimes it is difficult to know if you are just perceiving discrimination or racism, or if it is actual. I think African Americans on all White campus might experience the same dilemma. I don't think I have experienced anything worth giving any time or attention to.

Lindsay cannot target anytime that she has experienced overt discrimination but she has wondered whether or not she might have had discrimination or racism directed at her.

> I haven't experienced anything that I have sensed has been unspoken or subtle or could be of my own wondering if that could be the case. So, it could come out of not knowing or a perception I am not speaking of. There has been nothing at all overt that had anything to do with race. I think that there have been times when I have wondered if I had been African American would this experience been different but I have never asked that. I never spoke that and no one ever told me that. None of that is ever spoken so I don't know if I am generating questions of if it is subtle… In terms of employment, I have never been a minority except by gender…

Two participants were considerably cavalier about the subject, remarking that they "joke" and "have fun with it." Floyd (OU) was nonchalant as he spoke:

> Everyone is cool here. I'm cool. Nothing like that happens or happened, not to me. We joke about it sometimes; you know who you can joke with. Some people get it wrong; they misunderstand all the time, I think. No.

Bob laughed nervously as he recounted,

> I joke them a lot. I never had any racial discrimination. I have fun with it, I told [department chairperson] in the faculty meeting last fall... I want to file a complaint against [name withheld] he yelled at me 'Hey boy!' in the halls... I'm just kidding around but poor guy... I have never had that at all. I've never worked with a warmer more personal faculty than I have here.

Interestingly, Brad has experienced discrimination on campus at RC by other White men for his seemingly "liberal" attitude.

> I was like put in the office with another White male and they were perhaps a little bit iconoclastic... I don't feel like it was racial at all but I think it was more ideological; they might have been a real conservative republican or something and here I am. I consider myself to be a somewhat liberal democrat. I've always been, like, I voted for Jimmy Carter... I don't really feel like it has been racial I feel like it has been ideological, I think that there has been some differences, it's like I said I can get along with them 'cause the last two office mates that I had were White men that are total opposite of me. So, they put me in there I guess they figured that I could get along with them. So for me it is more ideological it hasn't been racial at all. I can get along well with my colleagues and I really don't even think about it so much when [for example] we are on the Spring Arts Committee together, whether or not my colleagues are Black or White. I think I may know more about whether they are conservative or real conservative to tread on thin ice or to be real careful like not to upset or like whatever you know.

Davis responded with a definitive "no" to the question of perceived racism or discrimination on campus. He did, however, entertain the ways in which he might have been perceived, himself, as engaging in discriminatory or racist acts. Davis discussed at length the importance of race and culture based sensitivity.

There may have been some times when as White faculty there is a tendency to not be as sensitive about things that are, from my perspective, not an issue. Of course when you're not accustomed to a particular culture it's a learning process, and perhaps the greatest difficulty on my end has been not only to learn what those sensitivities are and be aware of them but making sure that non-White faculty when they hear them or when I say them that they know that it is because I don't know and not because there is some underlying reference to perhaps a discriminatory background or from a racist standpoint. [Any insensitivity] is strictly coming from just I don't know and once of course I discover "oh, that's an issue" it's "I didn't know, I'm sorry." Much like if I didn't know anything about the Hindu religion and about how cows are sacred within that religion, you know, once you learn that you don't offer a Hindu a hamburger. It's kind of the same thing when you are trying to fit in you don't want to walk up and say "hey my nigga" because it is such a common phrase.

The researcher probed civilly, 'Do you say that to your White colleagues?" Of course not, but what is talked about is perhaps what we perceive as a double standard on how [the N-word] is tossed around so cavalier amongst African American students and faculty sometimes in their close quarters. Yet, it is very taboo for a person of my ilk to use the same phraseology even though there is no hostile intent meant by it. We view it as a term of endearment because that's the way we see it used but the word itself is so complex in how it's used so it is just best to not use it at all if you are not Black.

BEHAVIORAL DIMENSION

The behavioral dimension explored interactions both internal and external to the institutions examined in this study. Participant responses were categorized as collegial interactions and social interactions. Collegial interactions were characterized as institutional, but primarily departmental relationships with colleagues and students. Social interactions were distinguished as activities both academic and non-academic in nature.

Collegial Interactions

Collegial interactions were primarily viewed as "positive," "supportive" and "respectful" yet Lindsay, for example, felt "holding back… in a curious way" although she was careful to acknowledge her insecurities as a probable reason for this perception. Drew felt good about collegiality at OU with the exception of "some people." He does however feel that this "is the same everywhere." Patrick attributed tensions in collegial relations at RC as having to do with "agendas."

> I would describe collegial relations on this campus as strained. A lot of people have their own agendas and unfortunately we don't see the overall mission of the institution as the primary reason that we are here.

Cindy also described "strained" collegial relationships at RC but for different reasons.

> I think that the strain is only in certain areas. I feel like I fit in here, I don't feel out of place even though I'm White in a primarily Black setting. But I think some of the faculty and staff, don't, if they're White, don't feel like they fit in that well. Occasionally I've encountered a kind of strain, you know, in a colleague who is African American and I don't know, I'm not sure, like I said I've only been here four years and I still feel very new sometimes, so I'm not sure if that is coming from a racial, um, basis.

Brad considers himself "positive" and "non-confrontational." He has been described by his chairperson as a man who can "get along with the devil."

> And I really can 'cause I'm a non-confrontational person and I just like to move on, I've got these tasks that I want to accomplish you know or fulfill or these goals in my life that I want to fulfill, I am a very positive person.

Davis described collegial relations at his institution as ultimately an aggregate of co-workers united for the benefit of the same goal or "all in this together."

> Probably, this is a hard question to answer because you just never know truthfully how people see you, and you really kind of see yourself through other people without the benefit of knowing really what they are thinking, but on the surface I would have to say that it's respectful. They're respectful of my work as I am respectful for the most part of their work because we do work hard at this institution and the work it seems is endless, it's never done

and there's always a new, a new, challenge that presents itself daily that you have to overcome. So, there's an old saying that we're all accustomed to, 'we're all in this together' that would have to be the collective feeling of all faculty and staff here at this institution we're all in this together whether we want to realize it or not. Yes, we have issues from time to time with one another with how the business gets taken care of but essentially what you do have is, and I don't want to use the term family because I believe that it has been over used at this institution, but there is healthy respect for one another and what it is that we do.

Ben thinks that "collegial relationships on campus are for the most part good…"
> But there is a little bit of a hinge in there because if something goes wrong in a relationship and it is between somebody who is Black and White- the two people are Black and White- then I think race can very quickly get injected into it. So for the most part when people are doing their job well, they are just paying attention to doing business, I think people are collegial, they get along well and racial ethnicity doesn't play much of a role. But as soon as something goes wrong and there is the difference of Black and White then I think it is likely that that factor gets thrown into it. But that doesn't happen very much.

Ellen observed dynamics that should be considered when assessing collegial relationships between Black and White faculty.
> … cultures have their distinct way of interacting. I come from a whitewashed background and I may not know the culture or the language but I know people and I know how to be polite and respectful.

Faculty-Student Interactions

When asked whether they thought their ethnicity impacted faculty-student interactions, seven of those faculty members interviewed answered positively. By comparison, three faculty members responded that their ethnicity did not impact their relationships with students and two more faculty members were unsure. Ellen responded that "my gender and age seem to play a greater role in the way we communicate than my race. Like

Ellen, Ben thought race had no impact of his interaction with students but instead his being a man or an "older man" impacted dialogue with student more than race.

> I find that it's one of the beautiful things for me, I find that when I interact with classes, when I interact with individuals in my office, in my role now as Associate Dean, I find that my ethnicity has almost nothing to do with interactions. Sure, occasionally we talk about race and I will refer to myself as a White person and there may be some connection or some discussion of that but it is generally not a factor. I mean, I just interact with people and so I don't think about, I don't consider it to be a Black-White interaction. I consider it a person to person interaction. I'm much more aware of my being a man talking to students or being an older man talking to students than I am being a White man talking to students.

Drew also thought that ethnicity had little to do with impact but "personality" weighed heavily on interactions.

> Students perform better I think when they can relate to a professor but sometimes this has more to do with personality than ethnicity. Actually I think students relate more to the way you relate with them than what color your skin is.

Lindsay believes that, "Ethnicity always impacts interactions," elaborating on her rationale she continued,

> … So I don't think we can be color blind. I think that it can have a real positive impact I think that it broadens horizons for both people. For example when I am interacting with African American students it expands my cultural sensitivity and awareness because often there are cultural factors that are a part of the learning process…

Joan thinks that her ethnicity impacts both faculty-students interactions and student learning outcomes. During her interview she described in depth how her ethnicity as an instructor helps to prepare African American students to compete in a "White world" unlike perspectives they might get from an all Black faculty.

> One of the problems and we talk about this as a faculty is [OU] can be too nurturing. People can come to [OU], African-American students, and be very protected. They can study for 4 years and

then they graduate and they have to go out into a majority White world where the numbers are changing. However, in corporate America they are not changing, and if you go to work at many of the large corporations there are not a lot of people of color who are in upper management positions, still. So, our students have to compete in a world where after they have been at [OU] where you were the best, you were encouraged to be the best and people made some concessions for you because they understood some of the problems you might be having with your family, with your life, you don't have that same level of understanding when you go out into a workforce that's not as nurturing. Sometimes we do our students a disservice by making it such a nurturing place. We need to put the pressure on them so that they will be prepared. We talk about this a lot in faculty meetings and when we make decisions about requirements for courses about deadlines and things like that. We set a higher standard because we want our students to be able to compete once they leave this campus. I think probably it helps students; I may have a very different perspective on things. It probably helps students if I'm teaching a reporting class I'm going to teach what I know and what my experience was and that experience might be vastly different from [Black, Indian or Asian faculty members]. So, we teach what we know. So, for student learning that's a good thing because they're going to get different perspectives from each one of us that will help them when they go out into the real world. If they had all Black faculty they would not get that different perspective. So I think it is important. It helps them to get it, you know sometimes we'll be talking and they'll say, "You know I never realized that."

Brad thinks that his ethnicity is initially a shock to students who might have been expecting a Black instructor at an HBCU and find that he instead is the professor.

… I walk in there and some of the students are probably thinking like, 'my parents are paying all of this tuition' and you know here I am, here's this White guy walking in here, you know I've come to this school, a historical, an HBCU in [City, State] and it's like, 'What is this?! Look at this White guy. I could have gotten this in Toledo or Montgomery or anywhere.' And I think that immediately that all starts, I start giving them the syllabus and we start to talk and I think I just break the ice immediately… I think it really helps me because you know they are looking at me, looking at this guy going, 'You know this is a different experience,' 'Wow, this is really different,' 'Yea, this guy right here is definitely different.'

Brad enthusiastically shared how he uses his sense of humor and ethnicity to inspire student learning through reading.

I'm reading Michael Moore's *Stupid White Men* and my students love it when I tell them what it's about because here they are looking at me and here I am can talk about an ethnicity of which I am a part and I can make fun of them and go, 'Look, these are the serial killers, these are the guys you've got to watch out for,' you know and we are all laughing about it but it's true! But it really is true, and I think they appreciate that. What I do is that I recommend for them to read. I suggest to my students that if you're going to read Michael Moore then you must also read someone like Cornel West [named stated enthusiastically] because then you get the same issues. Of course amongst Whites, if you're talking among some White guys quote un-quote, especially like the FOX News audience those guys just go ballistic and if you just mention the name Michael Moore it is like you've pushed a button and they just go crazy but sure they've never read the book because a lot of what it says is like the same things Cornel West says, and he just gives you the statistics and that's like most people who commit crimes are White men and things like that are kind of interesting to know.

John also feels that students show up to the first day of class expecting to see someone other than a White instructor.

I would imagine that at least the first time they meet me, they are like 'who's this White guy that's teaching this class?' kind of thing. Again that is just what I imagine that they're thinking. Hopefully after a very short time and this works both ways- that I get to know them and they get to know me, I know when I look at a class- of course I can't sleep the night before anyway because it is the first day of a class, and they're just a bunch of faces regardless of the color of them, they are just a bunch of faces there, they are this class of people called students.

Davis likes to think that his ethnicity has no impact on student learning outcomes and believes that if it did have an impact there would be no viable means by which to measure such a factor. Davis hopes that his presence at the institution helps to "demystify" perceptions of Whites for students.

> I want to say that it has but there's no measurement for that. I like to think that it hasn't would probably be more correct. Whether it has or not I'm unsure of because there isn't a real measurement to know what the impact has been. Grades are really not a good measurement for it because if you're smart you're just smart and whether your instructor is Indian or they're Hispanic or if they're German or Italian or Black or White has no bearing on that necessarily. You're just a smart student that made an 'A.' ... I hope that having been an employee for so long as an instructor of the institution that I could help demystify how Whites are viewed by non-White individuals and there not be this fear of approaching or being able to talk. Perhaps there was a student who thought, 'oh wow, I really never thought that you were as down' as they say or as the students would say in their colloquial, their kind of vernacular not because of my knowledge or anything but just because of my personality and they didn't realize that White people could be so cool.

Patrick believes that while his initial reception by students may be negative, by the end of the semester "they see the value of diversity."

> In the beginning of a semester it may be very negatively because they wonder why they've come to an HBCU and have a White faculty member. By the end of the semester they see the value of diversity. And that comes through the interaction of me explaining my concepts and then explaining theirs back and we learn from each other.

Social Interactions

Social interactions occur between individuals and groups. Persons engaged in social interactions both assign meaning to a situation and interpret meaning from the situation, then conduct themselves accordingly. Faculty were asked to discuss their level of involvement on campus and any social activity beyond the institution's walls. Participants shared the intensity of their involvement on campus, in the classroom and in support of non-academic functions. Some participants discussed interactions with colleagues such as home visits and holiday parties. A few participants described their social interactions as primarily academic-related. Lindsay expressed that she was involved on campus to the limits of her professional obligations and felt she "was not included anyway" in social interactions.

> What determines the level of involvement is outlined in the particular job, for example, my involvement is the same as anyone else's. So involvement is according to level of expectations and committee and participation all the same for everybody...

Ellen feels that she is "involved enough."

> I'm not very involved but not because I am White... I dedicate a lot of time to research. I don't have time to get involved more than what is required of me... maybe things will change. I think I am involved enough.

Patrick described himself as "very involved on different levels" but did not speak so highly of his colleagues at RC.

> I think a large percentage of our faculty are very passive. I think they teach their classes, they fly under the radar and are very happy with being quiet.

Cindy is very involved on campus in academic and non-academic activities yet considers herself an anomaly among non-Black faculty.

> Frequently I think I'm very involved. I'm not the kind of person who can just teach my class and then say bye and then leave you at school... I have attended events that I think are fun and enjoyable for me to attend and they also show my students that I support them. Things like the Homecoming step show, I brought my kids for it and they really enjoyed the performances. Also, the Homecoming game and different things that probably the great majority of Black faculty might attend but not- probably few to none- of the non-Black faculty.

Davis is highly involved on campus but has felt that his input was not always well received. He discussed the nature of his interactions on campus in terms of the process by which they would often proceed and ultimately evolved.

I think initially the focus for me was just to become a good instructor, make sure I did my work. The extra-curricular activity would come later once I got into my comfort zone with having to teach at a historically Black institution as well as my interaction with other non-White faculty. Surprisingly, people are people, and when you have a shared experience or a common goal color does not become the dominating issue it is more or less ideology and ideas that become, than can become an issue. For the most part there are not any huge differences between what it is that I would come up with as an idea as opposed to what a Black faculty member or a non-White or a non-Black faculty member would come up with and if there was some disagreement that was okay. That was fine, we would come to some kind of compromise and meet each other half way but there was not any death threats, no kind of rock'em sock'em robot kind of confrontations, it was always what you would expect from a collegiate institution. There was always this respect when you walked into the room of everyone's opinion of what everyone's been talking about.

Ben described his observations on campus involvement by race.
... I think that most faculty White or Black get involved in the life of this university and get involved in the campus and contributions to the life of the campus is pretty much the same. I don't see many faculty holding back.

Those social interactions that occurred beyond the academic, administrative and professional confines of the institutions were not discussed by all faculty. Moreover the scope of those social interactions ranged from being political, festive, celebratory and domestic in nature as indicated in experiences shared by Joan who said,
As a matter of fact I am helping one of my colleagues to move on Friday. I'll be helping her to pack her clothes, carrying boxes.

Joan observes that faculty of different races "absolutely" interact with each on varying levels.
They party together, socialize together, serve as mentors to each other, do collaborative research together, projects together. I don't think there's anything that we don't do together.

Ben says, "The majority of the people I have had at home are probably

Black." He also has invited White professors to his home but who they are as people is what matters most to him. He thinks social interactions are not distinguished by race but has some hesitation. Ben explains,

> But at the same time when you say that, I am also aware that when I watch my Black colleagues interact there is something about being members of the community, members of the Black community which brings about a certain language a certain camaraderie which is different. It is like people being in the same fraternity or the same sorority. When they get together there is a certain kind of interaction which you can notice. So, I can see certain kinds of interactions which are culturally bound and which may involve Black colleagues. But even I having been here so long may even engage in some of that. Some of that camaraderie because I know the culture pretty well, I've been around it for a long time. So, for the most part race doesn't get into any social interactions. But occasionally you can see when just Blacks are together or even when just Whites are together you might see a certain style of interaction that might be typical to that racial group.

Similarly, Joan acknowledges the cultural nature of events yet believes colleagues are inclusive without emphasizing ethnicity.

> I've been to Kwanza parties. We don't struggle to say this is a Black thing and you need to come to it or this is an Asian thing. I think we do things that we would normally do and hopefully people would want to participate in if we are friends and colleagues and you want to support what people are doing as well.

Drew tends to acquiesce with the sentiment from most participants in this study of inclusiveness in social interactions.

> My colleagues have parties all of the time and everyone is invited. I am never excluded for being White. I just went to an Obama fundraiser two months ago that one of my colleagues hosted. Race has nothing to do with interaction.

Likewise, Ellen shared her observation,

> I see all kinds of faculty interacting. Ostin University is a melting pot of people and everyone seems to get along. African Americans might appear to socialize more but there are more of them, that's all, I mean it is an HBCU.

Ben, was the senior most faculty member interviewed in this study having
served his respective HBCU for almost a half century, 40 years. Summarizing his experience at Ostin University, Ben confided,

> Bottom line really has been, this experience has been, really I've
> been here for 40 years of my whole life and I am happy, I'm
> delighted, I'm close to retirement now and I'm thinking about it
> and one of my problems and anybody who knows me has heard
> me talk about it and knows is I am having a very hard time saying,
> "[Ben] what are you going to do if you're not at [Ostin University]
> talking to students, talking with people about their issues their
> problems whatever about grades, every day." And so I have found
> being a White person at a Black school that it's been a very
> satisfying experience and it's allowed for a lot of personal growth
> for me and I wouldn't give it up, I wouldn't change it for anything.

A FINAL WORD FROM FACULTY

Participants in this study were offered the opportunity to share their views on the topic in addition to any questions that may or may not have already been asked. Faculty augmented their significant responses submitted beforehand with suggestions for cultivating, respecting and nurturing diversity.

Joan willingly shared her thoughts with HWIs relative to cultivating a diverse faculty and ensuring the climate is welcoming.

> I think it is just important that people listen. You're going to have people come in with preconceived notions and so much of it is based on how you've been raised and who you've worked with. I think if we were a more open society, if we listened more before we just walked in and said whatever is on our chest that we'd be a much a better society for it. I think that there would be people who were much more happier in their professional lives as well as their personal lives. I think that we tend to carry too much baggage and some of it goes back years and years and there is nothing that we can do about that. Someone once said to me, and it is so important, 'words once they're said can never be dead.' You need to think about the things that you say to people because everyone has value and everyone has a story to tell and everybody can make a contribution if you give them an opportunity to do that.

Davis thinks that historically White institutions must first change their perspectives about HBCUs in order to receive the valuable lessons about adversity and diversity.

> There really needs to be real efforts by HWIs in understanding that there is much to be learned from an HBCU and not merely dismiss us as having been degree mills or less than competitive or any less serious about the academic programs that HBCUs engage in and there not be this air of superiority over HBCUs simply because it is Black. Once we can remove the facade of elitism from HWIs and look at this thing being a two way street, we learn from you, you learn from us, and there is something to be learned from HBCUs,… HBCUs are unique in not only their offerings but their instinct for survival their often, often, often overlooked contribution to society, um, sometimes I go online and read some

the different articles that always paint historically Black institutions with this wide brush as if we can connect them all into this one large canvas but it is so unfair because you know because predominately White institutions are not painted with that same wide brush... But I'm saying all of this to say that historically Black institutions should never apologize for the mission that they have set up from many decades ago; it should continue...

Brad shared his "great idea" about how to unite students from HBCUS and HWIs as a starting point for the purpose of inspiring dialogue and cultivating diversity across institutions.

I have an idea! I have a great idea. We are working on these community grants right now and I want to write one up to get the other, I'm going to Montevallo tomorrow for the writer's conference, and I want to get Montevallo, Samford, Birmingham-Southern, UAB, I want to get their students together with our students and meet at like one of these coffee houses downtown or something. I think that would be a good common ground. And to get our students to exchange, to read, to do spoken word together. And I think for them to start hearing some of these stories would do them a lot of good. That would be good.

When you meet your friend on the roadside or in the market place,
let the spirit in you move your lips and direct your tongue.
Let the voice within your voice speak to the ear of his ear;
For his soul will keep the truth of your heart
as the taste of the wine is remembered
When the colour is forgotten and the vessel is no more.

KAHLIL GIBRAN
on 'Talking' from *The Prophet* (1923)

8 WHITE FACULTY VOICED AND HEARD

This study investigated the racial climate at Historically Black Colleges and Universities (HBCUs). Twelve tenured/ tenure-track White faculty members were invited to share their experiences in making sense of their perceptions of HBCU campuses. As such, participants discussed their perceptions of diversity, campus involvement, collegial and faculty-student interactions. In addition, situations they encountered or perceived as discrimination or racial conflict were discussed.

This chapter is divided into four sections. The first section provides an overview of the study. The second section of this chapter presents a discussion and analysis of the findings in this study. Implications for policy and practice are explored in the third section, and the final section emphasizes recommendations for future research.

OVERVIEW OF STUDY

White faculty upon entrance at HBCUs must integrate into an organizational culture from which they emerge no longer as belonging to the hegemonic class but instead as 'minorities' in a majority Black population. As newcomers to the institution, they both affect and are affected by the environment within which they ideally seek to assimilate. Hurtado et. al. (1998) found that stakeholders demonstrate positive interactions and performance when the institutional culture is perceived as supporting diversity. Hence, the focus of this study was to gain insight into White faculty perceptions of racial climate at HBCUs.

Warnat (1976) found that there are several reasons explaining why White faculty might choose to work at HBCUs. Previous research also suggests that White faculty who teach at HBCUs encounter a wide range of experiences on a variety of levels (Foster, Guyden, & Miller, 1999; Smith & Borgstedt, 1985; Warnat, 1976). Still, others have introduced the nature of and impetus behind those experiences of White faculty at HBCUs. For example, the significance of faculty diversity at HBCUs was emphasized by Foster, Guyden and Miller (1999). Empirical research on White faculty at HBCUs is outdated, thereby necessitating a contemporary exploration of racial climate as perceived by White faculty at HBCUs.

Thus, this research study explored the perceptions of White faculty regarding their perceptions of racial climate at HBCUs. The primary research question of this study was: How do White faculty at HBCUs perceive racial climate? The secondary research questions were as follows:

1. How do they perceive the professional atmosphere at HBCUs?
2. How do they perceive the culture of HBCUs?
3. How do their perceptions of HBCUs change after starting employment at an HBCU?

In order to gain insight into the perceptions of White faculty at HBCUs, twelve tenured/ tenure-track faculty members at two four-year institutions participated in one, in-person interview. The two institutions were Ostin University (OU), a large private institution in an urban location in the North, and Rohan College (RC), a small private institution in a rural location in the South. All of the participants shared the following attributes: (a) White (Anglo-Saxon) descent, (b) teaching at an HBCU full-time and, (c) in a tenured/ tenure-track position with a Ph.D. degree.

Through the participants' shared experiences, both positive and negative, themes emerged relative to their perceptions of the racial climate. The positive themes were a welcoming environment, a diverse aggregate of faculty, constructive collegial relationships and comparable levels of faculty involvement. Conversely, participants identified the absence of intentional institutional initiatives to promote diversity, and racial discrimination was reported by a few participants. Still, optimistically, none were inclined to leave as a result.

DISCUSSION OF ANALYSIS AND FINDINGS

Based on the findings of this study, White faculty did not view the racial climate at HBCUs as antagonistic or estranged. Only one participant reported a direct encounter with racial discrimination from peers. Another reported discrimination indirectly as articulated in the language of a guest speaker. A third expressed a 'sense' that race played a role in promotion and tenure; however, he experienced no incident of prejudice himself. None alleged an experience so dire as to warrant distress or an exit from the institution. Although the limitations of this study constrain the generalizability of the findings, it does provide insight for implications for policy, practice and future research.

Perceptions of Professional Atmosphere

Prior experience is an important part of gauging subsequent encounters. Furthermore, background and sense of "ethnic identification" as belonging to a privileged class can affect perceptions, thereby an assessment of previous professional experience and personal development are vital to comprehending the context of White faculty perceptions.

Of those twelve participants interviewed in this study, only two reported a diverse personal background, one having a multicultural/ international upbringing and the other reported African American social peers with whom he 'partied' as an undergraduate.

Responding to the question of professional background, ten participants had only previous experience at an HWI; one worked only at an HBCU beforehand, and another had no experience at all before accepting a position at an HBCU. Primarily, participants in this study chose to work at an HBCU for want of a job. Judging from the large number of faculty disembarking from HWIs with employment as their only incentive to work at an HBCU it may be surmised that they are consistent with Warnat's (1976) 'moron' who seeks refuge at the allegedly inferior Black institution for reasons of incompetency among their social and professional peers. Three others saw the school in a dismal situation which they sought to remedy by assuming duty as university faculty. Having expressed their motivation, thus, is consistent with Warnat's (1976) conceptualization of the 'messiah' having come to save the wretched Black institution from the jaws of obliteration. Only two individuals came to the HBCUs in this study without prior experience as full time faculty at another institution. Perhaps, they may be the only examples of Warnat's (1976) 'marginal man.' Respecting the breadth of reasons White faculty may have for assuming a position at HBCUs, it stands confirmed that the professional atmosphere at HBCUs is perceived as receptive by White faculty who seek employment therein.

Diversity as an intentional institutional objective was maintained by half of the participants in this study. Of those faculty members, only two were able to provide some type of evidence to support their claim that faculty diversification at the institution was deliberate. This revealed that the tradition of inclusion and numerical stratification of faculty by race at HBCUs was sufficient to attract a diverse faculty and prompt their retention as supported by Johnson, Hoskins, Johnson, (2008). One faculty member noted the university mission statement as evidence of institutional initiatives to promote faculty diversity and two others indicated that departmental handbooks were evidence of institutional diversity efforts. Mandatory workshops and training on diversity were not reported by participants in this study; however, one faculty member did speak of an optional diversity course offered by the campus center for international affairs. Even so, initiating dialogue on diversity and instituting compulsory diversity training for all faculty at HBCUs may enhance campus climate for everyone involved.

Attitudes, perceptions and experiences at an institution are influenced by one's status as being an "insider" or an "outsider." White faculty at a majority Black institution are inclined toward perceptions of prejudice or discrimination due to their 'minority' status. Two participants reported direct incidences of discrimination and five others made observations on the topic of perceived or experienced discrimination on campus. Hypersensitivity to "language" usage among 'insiders,' paranoia, or "problematical" articulation of perceived issues is a consequence of being an 'outsider' as evidenced by a respondent who said,

> Sometimes it is difficult to know if you are just perceiving
> discrimination or racism, or if it is actual. I think African
> Americans on all White campus might experience the same
> dilemma.

Perceptions of racial tension can negatively affect psychological adjustment at an institution. However, consistent with Johnson, Hoskins, Johnson (2008) and Cabrera and Nora (1996), perceptions of discrimination were not an impetus for White faculty to depart from the institution. Adaptation is a critical component to the psychological adjustment for White faculty who perceived racial discrimination, indirectly, by learning to understand the norms, mores and colloquial speech of the majority population in order to provide an applicable and appropriate context to experiences.

Given the two participants who perceived discrimination as deliberately projected toward them, yet deemed it insignificant as to warrant attention suggests that HBCUs in this study maintain a positive environment. However, the collective number of participants reporting actual or perceived accounts of discrimination is sufficient to institute programs and policies on campus that address the issue of discrimination, thereby enhancing the racial climate and professional atmosphere for faculty.

The twelve participants in this study attributed their level of involvement to fulfilling the expectations of their faculty position. Two participants indicated that their colleagues were 'passive' in their commitment to departmental and institutional endeavors. Only one participant conveyed a desire to be involved beyond her professional expectations, and another expressed disinterest in extensive involvement on campus. Level of involvement is a reflection of the professional culture and the role one implicitly assumes within the institution. More specifically, the participants in this study might involve themselves only as they perceive the norm or according to their psychological role as a 'reverse minority' at a majority institution.

Interactions in this study were discussed as both academic, occurring between faculty and students, and extracurricular, such as social functions external to the university campus. Participants reported an atmosphere of positive engagement on both levels, yet conveyed a sense of personal "carefulness" and "caution." The historical legacy of inclusion and structural diversity at HBCUs contributed to the positive climate for professional and social interactions; however, paranoia inspiring feelings of apprehension stemmed from White faculty being 'outsiders.'

Consistent with Johnson, Hoskins, Johnson (2008), collegial relations were perceived as positive by White faculty at HBCUs. Nevertheless, some White faculty in this study experienced personal feelings of angst and concern regarding collegial interactions. Membership in departmental and institutional organizations and other such activities might facilitate the decline of personal insecurities among White faculty.

PERCEPTIONS OF CULTURE AT HBCUs

A historical legacy of inclusion was substantiated by the unanimous response from participants indicating sociohistorical references to the tradition at historically Black institutions and the contemporary climate on HBCU campuses. The historical legacy of inclusion on a campus has a positive impact on the cultivation of a supportive climate for 'minority' faculty, thus contributing to higher levels of satisfaction and a sense of community. White faculty assuming roles at HBCUs enter a supportive environment which has historically embraced an integrationist approach to professionalism and academia. A historical legacy of inclusion at HBCUs is confirmed by the Johnson, Hoskins, Johnson (2008) framework for assessing perceptions of racial climate.

Numerical representation of a diverse population on the HBCU campuses in this study is evident from statistics reporting a wide stratification of White faculty across disciplines. Structural diversity is critical to enhancing institutional climate. Together, the historical legacy of inclusion and structural diversity of those HBCUs explored in this study confirm a positive racial climate for White faculty at historically Black institutions. White faculty perceived the culture at HBCUs positively.

CHANGED PERCEPTIONS OF HBCUs

Participants in this study unanimously reported a positive change in their perceptions of HBCUs upon accepting a faculty position at their respective institution. Even the one faculty member who expressed feelings that her early exposure to diversity prepared her for entering a majority population as a reverse minority reported enhanced perceptions of the academic and social life at HBCUs upon being employed as faculty. Accordingly, the historical legacy of inclusion and diverse community of faculty at HBCUs create a nurturing environment for social and professional development.

IMPLICATIONS FOR POLICY AND PRACTICE

Themes identified across the two sites in this study can inform policy and practice about enhancing racial climate for faculty at HBCUs and HWIs. Commitment from administrators, faculty and staff is vital to establishment and institutional indoctrination of initiatives to improve racial atmosphere. It is necessary that policies be executed with clear objectives to facilitate inclusiveness, notwithstanding race or minority/majority populations, for whatever is the common good of all institutional stakeholders.

Institutions could cultivate a positive racial climate by developing programs that confront stereotypes and myths in order to reduce prejudice and strengthen organizational cohesiveness. Mandatory participation in institutional programs may promote interracial dynamics and ultimately organizational effectiveness. With the aim of enhancing climate, programs and policies inclusive of religion, gender, sexual orientation and other distinctive characteristics should be designed to engender diversity awareness and tolerance on campus. Faculty activities that foster informal interactions support heightened collegial and social interactions. Events that encourage engagements at regular intervals, particularly, can develop associations and might allay apprehension by faculty members.

RECOMMENDATIONS FOR FURTHER RESEARCH

The following recommendations for further research on racial climate at HBCUs are intended to expand current knowledge and advance insight into this phenomenon. Increasing the number of sites and participants in a future study on racial climate at HBCUs will extend the generalizability of the findings. Designing an instrument to provide a quantitative assessment of racial climate at HBCUs can be utilized to measure all faculty at HBCUs.

Augmenting the existing study with quantitative methodology will generate numerical representations of themes to supplement knowledge of research on racial climate. Studies on climate should be expanded to include diversity by gender, sexual orientation and religion in order to advance notions of inclusiveness on HBCU campuses. A study of the historical climate of HBCUs and the contemporary perpetuation of dated norms that emerge from a legacy of inclusion, however, prior to women's suffrage in the United States will explore diversity issues perhaps overlooked as a result of implied traditions. An assessment of climate as perceived by female/ male faculty of the 'majority' population at HBCUs might provide insight into the organization of a social and professional culture that can be generalized across Black female/ male interactions and relationships.

CONCLUSION

This study gives voice to a population that is absent from the literature on faculty at Historically Black Colleges and Universities. White faculty discussed their perceptions of racial climate at HBCUs. However, it is important to note that participants were often inconsistent with their responses, frequently contradicting positive statements with subsequent comments issued as an aside during or after the interview. Still, analysis of the findings revealed that overall, the racial climate at HBCUs was perceived as positive by White faculty. Conceivably, the historical legacy of inclusion at HBCUs and the structural diversity on historically Black campuses positively influenced White faculty experiences. Further research is necessary before detailed recommendations for policy, practice and research can be provided. Nonetheless, this study can be utilized to enhance campus racial climate at all institutions, particularly HBCUs and HWIs.

REFERENCES

Ahern, K. J. (1999). Pearls, pith, and provocation: Ten tips for reflective bracketing. *Qualitative Health Research, 9*(3), 407-411.

Allen, W.R. (1992). The color of success: African-American college student outcomes at predominately white and historically black public colleges and universities. *Harvard Educational Review, 62*(1), 26-44.

Allen, W.R. & Jewell, J.O. (2002). A backward glance forward: Past, present, and future perspectives on historically Black colleges and universities. *Review of Higher Education, 25*(3), 241-261.

Alexander-Snow, M., & Johnson, B.J. (1999). Perspectives from faculty of color. In R.J. Menges and Associates (Eds.), *Faculty in new jobs: A guide to settling in, becoming established and building institutional support* (pp. 88-117). San Francisco: Jossey-Bass.

American Association of University Professors [Electronic (1974). Version]. *Statement of Principles on Family Responsibilities and Academic Work*. Retrieved October 5, 2008 from http://www.aaup.org/statements/REPORTS/re01fam.htm.

Anderson, J.D. (1998). Training the apostles of liberal culture: Black higher education 1900-1935. In J.D. Anderson (Ed.), *The education of Blacks in the south 1860-1935*. Chapel Hill: University of North Carolina Press.

Anderson, T. P., & Lancaster, J. S. (1999). Building conversations of respect: The voice of White faculty at Black colleges. In L. Foster, J. S. Guyden & A. L. Miller (Eds.), *Affirmed Action: Essays on the academic and social lives of white faculty members at historically black colleges and universities* (pp. 165-174). Lanham, MD.: Rowman and Littlefield.

Antonio, Anthony, Lising (2003). Diverse student bodies, diverse faculties. *Academe, 89*(6).

Astin, A.W. (1991). Assessment for excellence: The philosophy and practice of assessment and evaluation in higher education. New York: Macmillan.

Astin, A.W. (1993). What matters in college: Four critical years revisited. San Francisco: Jossey-Bass.

Birnbaum, R. (1988). How Colleges Work. San Francisco, CA: Jossey-Bass.

Bishop v. Aronov, 926 F.2d 11th Cir. (1991).

Bogdan, R. C., & Biklen, S. K. (1998). Qualitative research in education: An introduction to theory and methods. Needham Heights, MA: Allyn and Bacon.

Bogdan, R. C. & Biklen, S. K. (2003) *Qualitative research in education: An Introduction to theory and methods* (4th ed.). Boston: Allyn and Bacon.

Bonnet, A. (2000). *White Identities.* Pearson Education.

Brown v. Board of Education of Topeka, 347 US 483 (1954).

Cabrera, A.F., & Nora, A. (1994). College students perceptions of prejudice and Discrimination and their feelings of alienation: A construct validation approach. *Review of Education/Pedagogy/Cultural Studies*, 16(3-4), 387-409.

Carnegie (2006). *The Carnegie Classification of Institutions of Higher Education.*

Cohen, A.M. (1998). *The Shaping of American Higher Education: Emergence and Growth of the Contemporary System.* San Francisco, CA: John Wiley & Sons, Inc.

Collins, P.H. (1986). Learning from the outsider within: The sociological significance of Black feminist thought. *Social Problems*, 33(6), 514-532.

Cooper, J. E., Massey, D., Graham, A (2006). Being "Dixie" at a historically Black university: A White faculty member's exploration of Whiteness through the narratives of two black faculty members. *The Negro educational Review*, 57(1-2).

Creswell, J. W. (1998). *Qualitative inquiry and research design: Choosing among five traditions.* Thousand Oaks, California: Sage Publications, Inc.

Creswell, J.W. (2003). *Research design: Qualitative, quantitative, and mixed method approaches* (2nd ed.). Thousand Oaks: Sage Publications.

Dawson-Smith, K. (2006) White faculty at historically Black colleges and universities. Ph.D. dissertation, University of New Orleans, United States Louisiana. Retrieved November 2, 2007, from Dissertations & Theses: Full Text database. (Publication No. AAT 3253090).

Dobbert, M. L. (1982). *Ethnographic research: Theory and application for modern schools and societies.* New York: Praeger.

Dow Chemical v. Allen 672 F.2d 1267 7th Cir. (1992).

Drzewiecka, J. & Wong, K. (1999). *Whiteness: The Communication of Social Identity.*California: Sage Publications.

DuBois, W.E.B. (1903, 2000). *The Souls of Black Folk: Henry Louis Gates, Jr. Editor.* W. W. Norton and Company: New York.

Dyer, R. (1997). *White.* New York: Routledge.

Elliott, P. G. (1994). *The urban campus: Educating the new majority for the new century.* Phoenix: Oryx Press.

Erickson, F. (1986). Gatekeeping and the melting pot. *Harvard Educational Review, 45,* 44-70.

Foster, L. (2001). The not-so-invisible professors: white faculty at the black College *Urban Education, 36*(5), 611-629.

Foster, L., & Guyden, J. A. (1998). *Content analysis of the viewpoints of selected White faculty members at HBCUs.* Paper presented at the Fifth National HBCU Faculty Development Network Conference. Miami, FL.

Foster, L., Guyden, J. A., & Miller, A. L. (1999). *Affirmed Action: Essays on the academic and social lives of White faculty members at historically Black colleges universities* (pp. 23-35). Lanham, MD: Rowman and Littlefield.

Franklin, J.H., & Moss, Jr., A.A. (1994). *From Slavery to Freedom A History of African Americans.* New York: McGraw Hill.

Gandy, O.H., Jr. (1998). *Communication and Race: A Structural Perspective.* Oxford University Press.

Glesne, C. (1999). *Becoming qualitative researchers: An introduction* (2nd ed.). New York: Longman.

Globetti, E.C., Globetti, G., Brown, C.L., & Smith, R.E. (1993). Social Interaction and multiculturalism. *NASPA Journal,* 30(3), 209-218.

Heintze, M.R. (1999). Black Colleges [Electronic Version]. Retrieved

7/22/2008 from
http:www.tsha.utexas.edu/handbook/online/articles/BB/khb1.html.

Hoffman, C.M. (1996). Historically Black colleges and universities: 1976-1994. Washington, DC: The National Center for Educational Statistics.

Huberman, A. M., & Miles, M.B. (2002). *The qualitative researcher's companion.* Thousand Oaks: Sage Publications.

Hurtado, S., Carter, D.F., & Spuler, A. (1996). Latino student transition to college. *Research in Higher Education,* 37(2), 135-137.

Hurtado, S., Milem, J. F., Clayton-Pedersen, A. R., & Allen, W. R. (1998). Enhancing campus climates for racial/ethnic diversity: Educational policy and practice. *The Review of Higher Education, 21*(3), 279-302.

Jackson, K.W. & Swan, L.A. (1991). Institutional and individual factors affecting Black undergraduate student performance: Campus race and student gender. In W.R. Allen =, E.G. Epps, & N.Z. Haniff (Eds.), *College in Black and White: African American students in predominately White and historically Black public universities* (pp. 127-141). Albany: SUNY Press.

Jewell, J.O. (2002). To set an example: The tradition of diversity at historically black colleges and universities. Urban Education, 37(1), 7-21.

Johnson, B.J., & Harvey, W. (2002). The socialization of Black College faculty: Implications for policy and practice. *The Review of Higher Education,* 25(3), 297-314.

Johnson, B. J., Hoskins, S.D., Johnson, T.E. (2008). *From Another Perspective: Faculty Perceptions- of the Racial Climate at Black Colleges.* Paper presented at the Annual Meeting of the Association for the Study of Higher Education (ASHE), Jacksonville, FL.

Leftwich v. Harris-Stowe State College 702 F.2d 686 (1983).

Levin v. Harelston 966 F.2d 85 2nd Cir. (1992).

Lincoln, Y. S., & Denzin, N. K. (1994). The fifth moment. In N. K. Denzin & Y. S. Lincoln (Eds.), *Handbook of qualitative research* (pp. 575-586).

Thousand Oaks, CA: Sage.

Lincoln, Y. S., & Guba, E. G. (1985). *Naturalistic inquiry*. Beverly Hills, CA: Sage.

Linton, R. (1939). *The study of man*. New York: Appleton-Century.

Manning, K. (1999). *Giving voice to critical campus issues. Qualitative research in student affairs*. University Press of America, Inc.

Marshall, C., & Rossman, G.B. (2006). *Designing qualitative research*. Sage Publications, Inc. McPherson, M. S., & Schapiro, M. O. (1998). *The Student Aid Game*. Princeton University Press.

Milem, J.F. (1998). Attitude change in college students: Examining the effect of college peer groups and faculty normative groups. *Journal of Higher Education*, 69(2), 117-140.

Miles, M. B., & Huberman, A. M. (1994). *Qualitative data analysis: An Expanded sourcebook* (2nd ed.). Thousand Oaks, CA: Sage Publications.

Nakayama, T., & Martin, J. (1999). *Whiteness: The Communication of Social Identity*. California: Sage Publications.

National Labor Relations Board v. Yeshiva University 44 U.S. 672 (1980).

Pascarella, E.T., Smart, J.C., Ethington, C., & Nettles, M. (1987). The influence of college on self-concept: A consideration of race and gender differences. *American Educational Research Journal*, 24, 49-77.

Pascarella, E.T., & Terenzini, P.T. (1991). *How college effects students: Findings and insights from twenty years of research*. San Francisco: Jossey-Bass.

Poole, M.S., & McPhee, R.D. (1983). A structurational analysis of Organizational climate. In L.L. Putnam & M.E. Pacanowsky (Eds.), *Communication and organization: An interpretive approach*. Beverly Hills: Sage.

Poole, Seibold, & McPhee (1997). Structuration of Group Decisions (p. 121). California: McGraw Hill Higher Education.

Porter S. (1993) Nursing research conventions: Objectivity or obfuscation? *Journal of Advanced Nursing*. 18, 137-143.

Redinger, M. A. (1999). You just wouldn't understand. In L. Foster, J. A. Guyden & A.L. Miller (Eds.), *Affirmed Action: Essays on the academic and social lives of White faculty members at historicallyBblack colleges and universities* (pp. 23-35). Lanham, MD: Rowman and Littlefield.

Robinson, Randall (2000). *The Debt: What America owes to Blacks.* The Penguin Group.

Roebuck, J. B., & Murty, K. S. (1993). *Historically Black colleges and universities: Their place in American higher education.* Westport, CT: Praeger Publisher.

Rossman, G., & Rallis, S. (2003). *Learning in the filed: An introduction of qualitative research* (2nd ed.). Thousand Oaks, CA: Sage Publications.

Rubin, H.J., & Rubin, I.S. (1995). *Qualitative interviewing: The art of hearing data.* Thousand Oaks: Sage Publications.

Scheerhorn, D., & Geist, P. (1997). *Social Dynamic in Groups* (p. 83-103). New York: Houghton Mifflin Company.

Slater, R. B. (1993). White professors at Black colleges. *The Journal of Blacks in Higher Education, 1,* 67-70.

Smith, S. L. (1982). *Dynamics of interracial relationships involving White faculty in Black colleges: Review, systemization, and directives.* Paper presented at the Annual Meeting of the Council for Social Work Education.

Smith, S.L., & Borgstedt, K.W. (1985). Factors influencing adjustment of White faculty in predominately Black colleges. *Journal of Negro Education,* 54(2).

Spaights, E., & Farrell, W. (1986). The enigma of the urban university. *Education, 106*(4), 356-352.

Stewart, C.J., & Cash, Jr., W.B. (2006). *Interviewing: Principles and practices.* New York: McGraw-Hill.

Strauss, A. & Corbin, J. (1990). *Basics of qualitative research: Grounded theory procedures and techniques.* Newbury Park, CA: Sage Publications. The Tradition of White Presidents at Black Colleges. (1997). *The Journal of Blacks in Higher Education, 16*(1), 93-99.

Thelin, J.R. (2004). *The history of American higher education*. Baltimore: The Johns Hopkins University Press.

Tierney, W. G., & Rhoads, R. A. (1994). *Faculty socialization as a cultural process: A mirror of institutional commitment* (No. 93-96). Washington, DC: George Washington University, School of Education and Human Development.

Tinto, V. (1993). *Leaving college: Rethinking the causes and cures of student attrition* (2nd ed.). Chicago: University of Chicago Press.

Tracey, T.J., & Sedlacek, W.E. (1985). The relationship of noncognitive variables to academic success: A longitudinal comparison by race. *Journal of College Student Personnel, 26*, 405-410.

Urban, W.J., & Wagoner, J.L., Jr. (2004). *The American education: A history (3rd ed.)*. New York: McGraw-Hill.

Warnat, Winifred, I. (1976). The role of White faculty on the Black college campus. *The Journal of Negro Education, 45*(3).

West, Cornel. (1993). *Race Matters*. Vintage Books: New York.

Woodson, Carter, G. (1990). *The Mis-Education of the Negro*. Africa World Press, Inc. Edition.

United States Department of Education (1996). *HBCUs: 1974 to 1994*. Washington, DC: US Department of Education. National Center for Education Statistics.

United States Department of Education (2004). National Center for Education Statistics, Integrated Postsecondary Education Data System (IPEDS), Winter 2001-02.

United States Department of Education, National Center for Education Statistics (2006). Digest of Education Statistics, 2005 (NCES 2006-0303), Chpt 3.

United States Department of Education (2008). http://www.ed.gov/about/inits/list/whhbcu/edlite-index.html. White House Initiative of Historically Black Colleges and Universities.

Webster's New College Dictionary (2008). Houghton Mifflin Harcourt, 3rd edition.

ABOUT THE AUTHOR

Dr. SaFiya Dalilah Hoskins is a communications consultant and founder of Ubiquitous Press. Previously, she was a director at a university and host of the talk radio show *Beauty, Brains and the Bottom Line with Dr. Sa* on a nationally syndicated radio network.

Dr. Hoskins earned her Bachelor of Arts Degree in Journalism with an emphasis in Public Relations and a minor in African American Studies from Howard University, her Master of Arts in Communication and Culture with an Organizational Communication focus, also, from Howard University; and, a Doctorate of Philosophy in Urban Higher Education and Educational Leadership from Jackson State University. Dr. Hoskins has worked in academe for over fifteen years and industry for twenty. She has held positions at Miles College, Bowie State University, Howard University, American University, Radio One, Def Jam Recordings, Black Entertainment Television (BET); and, as a director of communications at a non-profit organization. In addition, Dr. Hoskins has served on Capitol Hill in the office of Illinois Congressman Bobby L. Rush (D) and as Associate Producer to AWARE: Positive Health Talk Radio.

Dr. Hoskins' empirical research focuses upon the analysis of race, gender and class in American Society and the role of communication in social and organizational contexts. Her presentation of research on *White Faculty Perceptions of Racial Climate at Historically Black Institutions* with Dr. Barbara J. Johnson was well received by an international audience at The Association for the Study of Higher Education Annual

Conference. Dr. Hoskins has also been invited to present her research by the American Association of Blacks in Higher Education (AABHE) and the National Association for African American Studies (NAAAS).

Dr. Hoskins grew up in a culturally rich environment where creativity was nurtured and expression was encouraged. She published her first novel, *An Infrequent Pairing* under the name SaFiya Dalilah and was a featured poet in the anthology, *Alternatives to Surrender*. Dr. Hoskins is a regular contributor to the Harvard University, *African American National Biography*, Dr. Henry Louis Gates, Jr. and Dr. Evelyn Higginbotham-Brooks, editors; having written nearly seventy entries. Dr. Hoskins is the coauthor of *Growth and Development for the Millennial Generation* (with Wallace 'Gator' Bradley and Dr. Cornel West); and, she is the author of two children's books, *Binky: The Cutest Kitten Ever* and *The Adventures of Bouki and Rabby: Cottage in the Clouds* a Bahamian folktale (with Durelle Williams). Dr. Hoskins is the editor of *Altruism at HBCUs: Cultivating Institutional Relationships to Positively Impact Alumni Giving*; and, coauthor of the forthcoming nonfiction title, *Invasion of Privacy: Hacking the Celebrity Code* (with Calvis Robinson). She appeared in a series of two regional commercials for the play *Smilin' Faces* and was a featured guest of Chef Emeril Lagasse on the Discovery Channel Network's program *Emeril Green* in the episode, *Vexing Vegetarian*.

Dr. Hoskins enjoys writing, travel and music. She earned a certification to Teach English as a Foreign Language and relocated to Paris, France where she tutored children of West African descent; also, she traveled to Hong Kong, China as part of an international delegation to explore communication across cultural contexts. She has been a member of the Association for the Study of Higher Education (ASHE), American Educational Research Association (AERA), American Advertising Federation (AAF) and Public Relations Society of America (PRSA).

Dr. Hoskins currently resides in Washington, DC with her Maine Coon, Assata Elaine.

www.UbiquitousPress.com

Also on Ubiquitous Press:

Altruism at HBCUs: Cultivating Institutional Relationships to Positively Impact Alumni Giving

Murder to Excellence: Growth and Development for the Millennial Generation (The Autobiography of Wallace 'Gator' Bradley)

Study Guide for Murder to Excellence: Growth and Development for the Millennial Generation (The Autobiography of Wallace 'Gator' Bradley)

The Adventures of Bouki and Rabby: Cottage in the Clouds (a Bahamian Folktale)

Binky the Cutest Kitten Ever

To contact SaFiya D. Hoskins, Ph.D. email:
1DrSaFiya@gmail.com